WE PLAN, GOD LAUGHS

WHAT TO DO WHEN LIFE HITS YOU OVER THE HEAD

Sherre Hirsch

Doubleday

New York   London   Toronto   Sydney   Auckland

To my mother

DD
DOUBLEDAY

Published in the United States by Doubleday, an imprint of The
Doubleday Publishing Group,
a division of Random House, Inc., New York.
www.doubleday.com

A hardcover edition of this book was originally published in 2008
by Doubleday.

DOUBLEDAY is a registered trademark and the
DD colophon is a trademark of Random House, Inc.

Library of Congress Cataloging-in-Publication Data
Hirsch, Sherre.
We plan, God laughs : 10 steps to finding your divine path when
life is not turning out like you wanted/
Sherre Hirsch.
p. cm.
1. Self-actualization (Psychology) 2. Self-actualization
(Psychology)—Religious aspects—Judaism. 3. Fate and
fatalism—Religious aspects—Judaism. 4. Providence and
government of God—Judaism. 5. Planning.
6. Self-management (Psychology) I. Title.
BF637. S4H58 2008
296.7—dc22
2007034499

ISBN 978-0-385-52362-2

PRINTED IN THE UNITED STATES OF AMERICA

Contents

CONTENTS

AUTHOR'S NOTE

ON THE USE OF THE WORD "GOD"

For the sake of ease of reading, I have decided to use the male pronoun "he" in referring to God. In no way does this mean that I believe God is anthropomorphic with either male or female characteristics. I would never presume to assign a gender to God.

ON THE USE OF THE WORD "TRADITION"

Judaism is replete with traditions. It begins with the Torah, the five books of Moses, but it continues to be enriched and deepened over the centuries with the

Mishnah, the Talmud, the Midrash, and thousands of commentaries. Together these works form the foundation and heart of our people and our way of life. When I mention the "tradition," it is this body of work that I am referring to.

On the Text

In the interest of privacy I have changed some names and details in the real-life stories I tell. Also, when referring to the Bible throughout I am referring to the Hebrew Bible.

INTRODUCTION

MY MOTHER'S STORY

Today is not turning out like I wanted. Yesterday did not, and I imagine tomorrow will not either.

I dedicated this book to my mother because it was from her that I first learned that life does not go as planned. It was from her that I learned that it is never too late, that there is always something more, something better. I have carried this lesson with me every day of my life. It has sustained me when my life has not gone as I wanted. It has helped me counsel others. It has helped me be a better me, a better daughter, wife, mother, rabbi.

My mother was a small-town girl from London, Ohio. Her father died when she was eight. She was one of five kids being raised by a single mother. All she ever wanted was to get out, and at fifteen, she met my father. He was from the big city of Dayton and had everything she wanted: two parents, big house, family dinners. She thought she'd met her knight in shining armor. Things were finally on target to go as she'd planned.

They married when she was nineteen. She was a mother of two by twenty-four. When they decided to move to Los Angeles and my father started to succeed in his own business, it was everything she'd ever dreamed of.

But secretly, something did not feel right to her. It was what she'd thought she always wanted. Why wasn't she happy and fulfilled? She and my father started to fight more and more. They argued about money, parenting, the business. The downward slide was slow at first. He got angry at her and at the world. His personality seemed to change. What at first had seemed fiery and passionate started to feel scary and abusive. My father went into a deep depression. He abandoned the business and eventually refused to get out of bed. He literally lay there, expecting my mother to wait on him day and night.

They had bills to pay, children in private school,

a lifestyle to maintain; she had to go to work. What would she do? She had never balanced a checkbook. She had dated only one man, my father. Her sole job had been as a substitute teacher.

A Nordstrom was opening in our neighborhood. With no experience, my mother talked her way into a job as a sales assistant. She was in her late thirties learning how to work a computer for the first time. Within a year, she was promoted. The better her life at work got, the worse her home life became. My father grew more abusive. He demeaned her, insulted her, and even hit her.

She couldn't leave. Divorce was not part of the life story she had written for herself. My brother and I encouraged her to go. We lived in fear of our father. We never knew what would set him off. We were afraid of staying. Yet she was afraid of leaving.

But she continued to excel at work. She had discovered her passion. She loved making people look on the outside like they felt on the inside. Within two years, she became a senior personal shopper. Because she knew that everyone is beautiful, everyone loved working with her.

Four years into her new career, my mother became one of the leading salespeople in her company. Even though my father was continually tearing her down, she began to emerge and see that beauty was not only in others, it was within her. She began to find her authentic self. She began to discover this beautiful, strong, confident woman within her.

In her early forties, once my brother and I were in college, she finally left my father. She walked out the door with one suitcase and no money and headed to the neighbors'. She did not know where she was going or what would happen next. But she was not going back. As she was walking alone down the street, she thought, "This is not what I planned."

This life was not what my brother and I had planned either. At twenty and eighteen, we discovered that our father had incurred debt in our names. Not only were we on our own but we were being chased by the IRS. Every college semester when the bills were due, we prayed. We each found a way to survive. It was hard, but we were the lucky ones. What did we know? We were just starting out.

My mother, on the other hand, was not. She spent the next ten years rebuilding her life. She moved into a small apartment on a tight budget. She threw herself into her work and into making a living. With each step she became more and more empowered. Instead of waiting for the next promotion, she asked for one and got it. She began to take charge of her own life. She began dating. She started a group for divorced women. She started working out. Even though everything was new and a little uncomfortable, she kept moving forward.

She began to imagine her life as a successful, single career woman. A woman who discovered her inner strength and brought it to the world. She did not foresee where the plan would go next. So when she met Mort, a confirmed bachelor, she did not pay much attention. He did not fit into her new life plan. She had no intention of wasting time with someone who could not commit.

They dated casually for years. Her life was full, she had made wonderful friends, she loved her job, and she was traveling in her free time. So when Mort proposed, she was afraid to say yes. It was another leap. Her life was good. But she had learned in all those years that, by taking a step, she could change her life. She leapt.

When I officiated at their wedding, my mother wore my wedding dress. What I said then under the chuppah was that, at her first wedding, she was waiting for someone to rescue her. But at this wedding, she had rescued herself. She had taught us all that to live the life you want you have to be willing to leap. You have to be willing to realize that your life is not scripted. The happy ending starts with you.

WE PLAN, GOD LAUGHS?

We have all heard the Yiddish proverb "We plan, God laughs" (*Mann traoch, Gott läuch*), and every time we see on it on a bumper sticker, we laugh too because we know it is true.

We all have plans. With each stage of life, we imagined who we would be when we "arrived." But when we got there, things were not quite in place. Life did not turn out like we expected. In fact, at times life seemed to take another direction entirely. For a lot of us, it felt like we failed. We did not measure up. We were not who we thought we would be. Life was not turning out like we planned.

I remember my first plan. It was the Cinderella plan. I was going to become a beautiful princess. Then one day my fair and handsome prince would save me from my regular existence. We would fall in love with one magical kiss and live happily ever after. At the time the details were foggy, but the plan was in place. As I matured, the elements of fantasy disappeared, but the dream remained. One day I would fall in love with a wonderful man, get married, have 2.5 children, a house, a dog, and live happily ever after.

I never thought about what would happen if the plan did not go as planned. What if I did not meet the prince? What if the prince was really a frog? What if I could not have children? What if housing prices were too high? What if I was allergic to dogs? What if I discovered that this plan was not for me after all? What would happen if this plan didn't work? My fantasies were not necessarily based in reality.

I have learned this lesson over and over. When I was sixteen, my family spent a week white-water rafting. On the first day I fell madly in love with our guide. He was a teen's dream: a cool, tall, tan nature man. I wanted to spend the rest of my life on that raft trip, camping, cooking, and sleeping under the stars. It all seemed perfect on the first day. He could quote Thoreau. He could make elaborate dinners on a camping stove. He could lead me around the world on a boat. By the third day I learned he knew only one quotation by Thoreau. Chili was his masterpiece. I get seasick on boats. The smaller the boat, the more severe the illness. By the end, covered in bug bites, exhausted from the experience, starving for the city, a hot meal, and my comforter, I'd realized nature life was not all I had imagined it to be.

Just last week I got stuck in the trap again. Before I got married, I had fantasies of Shabbat dinner at our home. We would sit down perfectly dressed at a beautifully set table with flowers, with candles, with the aroma of a gourmet meal wafting through the house. As a mother of three small children, I have found out that if we can all manage to sit together at the table for five minutes, it is a miracle. We use paper plates because glass shatters. We use plastic tablecloths because wine stains. The candles can never be on the table because my children are little pyromaniacs. And our favorite smell is pizza. So when a Shabbat dinner goes especially wrong, like ours did just last week, it can seem symbolic of something much bigger. Is my marriage in trouble? Do we have "problem" children?

You would have thought that in adulthood (having realized that dogs give me hives and apartment rent in Los Angeles surpasses that of most castles) I would have let go of my improbable fantasies and root myself in reality. Even though "I knew," I still got angry.

It felt like God was laughing at me. He was making a mockery out of my life.

If God and I both knew that Cinderella was not real, why was I still waiting for my "happily ever after"?

> *What was your first plan?*
> *Are you still waiting for your happily ever after?*

Happily Ever After?

It never occurred to me that God might be waiting for his "happily ever after" too. God too may feel that some of his plans have not gone as he wanted and that we were laughing at him. It all started with Adam and Eve. They had only one rule, and they broke it. Cain killed Abel. The Israelites begged to return to Egypt. Moses broke the first set of the Ten Commandments. God plans, we laugh.

Sometimes literally. Sarah was ninety and Abraham was one hundred when God promised them a son. He said to Abraham, "I will give a son through her [Sarah], I will bless her and she shall give rise to nations." Abraham had no doubt. Like all men, he imagined he would be virile until he was a thousand. He was overjoyed. He laughed out of sheer happiness.

Sarah, on the other hand, was more realistic. She knew the odds of getting pregnant at ninety were zero. Just the thought of carrying a child at her age made her laugh. But her laughter was not the same as Abe's. She laughed mockingly at herself, her husband, and at God. She said, "After I have withered shall I again have delicate skin? And my husband is old!" She was not about to run out and decorate the baby's nursery.

God was angry. Sarah was laughing at him. No one had ever laughed at God. But of course she was laughing at him; all women would have, his plan was ridiculous. But God, angry or not, "remembered" her. God gave Sarah and Abraham a son in their old age. God commanded them to name him Isaac, meaning "laughter."

God has a sense of humor. With the birth of Isaac, God claimed the true meaning of laughter. Laughter was possibility, not mockery. Laughter came to represent joy, creation, love, faith, and passion. The tradition teaches that on the day Isaac was born there was so much of this new laughter in the world that women who had previously been barren gave birth.

People who had been sick were healed. On that day, the day of Isaac's birth, the world was filled with true joy. It was filled with laughter.

Emet's Plan

Each night when my husband and I pray with our son, Emet, he tells us his plans.

Emet is four. Some nights he will be a fireman, some nights a pirate, and some nights a doctor, which always makes his Jewish mother happy. When he falls asleep, my husband and I laugh together. In these moments we truly understand the proverb. God is not laughing at us, just like we are not laughing at Emet. Jeff and I are laughing with God.

We are celebrating this extraordinary creation. We are rejoicing in the potential of this child whom the three of us made together. It is the greatest feeling that our son can dream and achieve beyond what we think is possible. We love that for Emet the world has no limits. He inspires us, and I like to think that he also inspires God.

It may seem silly that my son's pirate dreams are in-

spiring to God, but inspiration often comes from unexpected places. One of the most amazing stories of
the entire Jewish tradition starts with the discussion
of an oven. Yawn. Essentially, the rabbis wanted to
know whether, if you placed an impure substance, say
a pepperoni pizza, in this particular oven, you could
still use the oven. One guy—Rabbi Eliezar—said yes,
everyone else said no.

Rabbis love to argue. No matter how much Rabbi
E tried to convince them, they were unswayed. Once
he realized that words would not be enough, he
started to perform miracles to show the superior-
ity of his opinion. He made a tree move. A stream
flow backward. The walls of a study hall shake. But
the other rabbis would not budge. Rabbi E decided
to use a last resort to convince them; he called God
himself. A voice descended from heaven and agreed
with Rabbi E. You would have thought at this point
the others would have deferred to his opinion.

Instead Rabbi Yehoshua turned to Rabbi Eliezar and
said, "In matters of everyday life, the majority rules,
not God." God knew from destruction—locusts, floods,
pillars of salt—this was bound to cause a pretty dramatic reaction. Zeus would have sent a thunderbolt in
an instant.

But God's reaction was extraordinary. God smiled. With laughter he said, "My children have overcome me." God was not resentful or vengeful. He was proud. He realized that his children were growing up. They were taking responsibility. His laughter in that moment was out of joy and love that his people were building upon his initial creation. God laughed because he was deeply moved.

We plan, God laughs. I misunderstood. It turns out that God is not mocking me. He is not looking at me with derision. Instead of smiling when I fall down, God has been smiling when I get up.

God loves my plans from Cinderella onward. God wants me to dream and to believe that I can become more, and he wants me to take action and move forward. God wants me to continue to enrich his creation. God wants me to have faith in my plans. God wants me to laugh.

So why is it so hard?

Why am I stuck?

Why are my plans not going as planned?

How come I am not laughing?

USING THIS BOOK

"Finding your divine path" sounds huge. It feels like
a lifetime's worth of work. But "following ten steps"
sounds almost too easy. The truth is, this guide falls
somewhere in between. Some of you may read the
steps in one night. Others may read a step a day, a
step a week, even a step a month. Regardless of
how you use this book, the steps will work. You
do not have to master each step. This is not a test;
it is a practice. Let yourself revisit the steps again
and again. Do not let your first impression be your
last. Realize that each step takes time to become
internalized. You will see that, with a little desire,
faith, and effort, your life can be transformed. You
can live the life you dream.

Everyone deserves to live the life they imagine and
you are no exception. Don't be too hard on yourself.
Don't think if tomorrow you do not wake up in a
new life that you are a failure. You are anything but.
Just for turning this page, God is smiling on you.

WE PLAN,
GOD LAUGHS

WHAT HAPPENED?

STEP ONE

The irony of the first step is that you do not go
forward, you go back. It is what you least expect
when trying to move forward. If you are anything
like me, there are times on which you would prefer
not to look back. But here you are. It's time to
ask yourself: What happened? How did I get here?
What led me to this moment? Was there a crisis?
A realization? Or did I just wake up wishing I was
someplace else?

The first step is always the hardest, for you must be
completely honest. It is easy to lie to yourself. It
is even easier to just breeze through this step. But
this one is the basis for all the others; that is why it

is first. The more effort you exert here, the more rewarding and meaningful the path will be.

∾

"This was not the plan."

As I sat there holding Brenda's hand, I couldn't speak. There were no words. What could I say? You are right, this is not the plan. It was better to stay silent. "She was supposed to take the SATs, go to the prom, go to college, marry a nice guy, have babies, become a grandma. This is not right. This is not fair."

It wasn't fair. It wasn't right. We cried together.

The last time I saw bubbly sixteen-year-old Katie, she'd stopped by my office on her way to summer break. "Hey, Rabbi, have a good summer."

"You too," I shouted back. "Any fun plans?"

"The usual, surfing, boys, camp, hanging out."

"Sounds good. Hey, come visit me here at the synagogue once or twice. I will be bored without you."

"I'll try."

Then she was gone.

Now in the waiting room of the hospital, hearing the prognosis, I knew the life she'd planned was gone for good.

Less than twenty-four hours earlier, Katie was a

teenager. Out with her friends for a night on the town. Not drinking, not partying—simply hanging out. Just like teenagers do. The love of her life was driving fast. Of course he was trying to impress her. But suddenly, he lost control, and the car flipped and then flipped again. He walked away. Now the doctors were saying Katie might die. If she lived, she would be a vegetable. She would never speak, walk, recognize her parents, laugh.

Two years later she is still living, if that is what you call it. Everyone else has left. Gone to the prom, to college, to Europe. Katie is still here, and I am still holding her mother's hand listening as she says, "This is not what I planned."

As a rabbi, time and time again I have heard, "This is not what I planned." "This is not fair." "This is not what I wanted."

The first time I met Michele and Rob, I was thinking, "This is how it is supposed to be." They were an adorable couple from day one. Totally in love. Two peas in a pod. Beshert, meant to be. Under the chuppah, it was clear the future looked bright. They had wonderful families, shared values, great chemistry, stable careers. A house filled with the laughter of children would be right down the line.

Two years later, when I got the call that they were pregnant, I was delighted. It was all going as planned. Michele kept me posted on the details. With each passing month, she would e-mail with glee. "I am getting bigger." "It's a boy." "He moved." "We saw his ears on the ultrasound." With all her reporting, and minute-by-minute details, I was getting pretty excited. Two weeks before the due date, Michele confirmed my availability for the bris (the ritual circumcision). "All set, on my calendar, no worries," I replied.

Two weeks passed to the day, and my cell phone rang. It was D-day. I answered, and there was silence.

"Hello . . . hello?" Something stopped me from saying "Mazel tov" (congratulations). It was the silence, the breathing, the echo of tears. "Are you all right? Is the baby okay?"

"No." Silence. "He is dead."

"Where are you? I am coming now."

When I walked into the hospital, I learned that in the past twenty-four hours, their baby boy had stopped moving. The umbilical cord had wrapped around his tiny neck and strangled him to death. He was full term. He was perfect. But nothing was perfect. We sat together, and we wept.

No one was immune from tragedy. Children were

born sick. Spouses were critically injured. Single parents lost their jobs. Every day I was reminded that life was not going like we planned.

BEFORE AND AFTER

For Brenda, Michele, and Rob, life was divided into "before" and "after."

The before was now idealized. And the after, the present, was weighing them down. In the initial shock, their friends and family rallied. They comforted them with food and with calls. Then, over time, everyone else's life returned to normal. But in their own lives, normal as they knew it no longer existed. They could not return to their former lives. Over time, they resigned themselves. Their "new normal" was now their reality, and that reality was not so great. For that reality was defined by a tragedy.

Some people struck by tragedy feel that they have been singled out. Angela was a terrific mom by all standards. It was her profession. She raised two beautiful children who grew up, went to college, got married. Her friends would ask her, "What is the secret?

What do I need to do?" Inside she would smile; she believed she was lucky. God was smiling down on her. She was blessed.

One day, out with her daughter and granddaughter, Angela noticed her daughter wincing. She asked, "Are you okay?"

"I have a stitch in my side, no big deal."

Just to be sure, they had it checked out. The doctors found nothing. But the pain continued, and less than a year later they had a diagnosis, a rare disease that would kill her within the year. Thirty-two, married, mother, dying?

Angela could not believe it. It is not natural. You do not outlive your children. The family banded together. They fought and fought. They consulted doctors, sought healers, did alternative treatments. You name it, they tried it. Six months later, Angela's daughter died in her mother's arms.

Angela keeps asking herself over and over, "What did I do to deserve this? What could my daughter have done? Is God out to get me?"

Fanny asked the same questions. She and Mel were Holocaust survivors. They had endured the concentration camps, the internment camps, the Russian occupation of Poland. They had immigrated to the

United States with only the clothes on their backs. But they had a dream. They would make a life here and not just survive but thrive. They did.

They worked hard. They saved their money. They lived simply. With each year, they invested their savings scrupulously. They had a plan—when they were sixty-five, they would retire, travel, enjoy life. Everything was set.

At sixty-five, they both retired with a lovely home, healthy children, beautiful grandchildren; it was now their time. They made plans to see the world. One night, Fanny called to Mel and he did not answer. She called again. No answer. Annoyed, she ran to the top of the stairs, only to find her husband lying dead in the foyer. He'd had a heart attack only minutes before. Their dreams vanished in an instant.

For both Fanny and Angela, before was now a distant memory. Their after felt like a life sentence.

THE DEATH OF DREAMS

People came to talk to me with all kinds of plans that had gone awry. Not all the stories were exceptional but they still mattered. They came to talk to me because they knew I understood. Maybe they felt a kinship. I was not embarrassed to reveal my own disappointments, big and small. I had realized that I was not alone, and when they came to me, I let them know that they were not either.

My first impression of Joan was that she was deflated. I soon learned why. In high school, Joan had been a superstar. Valedictorian, captain of the cross-country team, vice president of her class. It was not a surprise when she won an academic scholarship to a prestigious university. She had a plan. She would become a research physician working with children with rare diseases.

But two years shy of Joan's graduation, her mother was diagnosed with brain cancer. Joan was the only sibling without her own children, so the burden of care fell to her. She dropped out of college. Two years later, her mother died, and so had her scholarship. Saddled with debt, Joan had to go to work. College was no longer an option. But without the degree, her career choices were limited. Now, in her thirties, her dreams seem even more unattainable. She feels she is too old to go back to college and start again, so she continues to plug away at her day job just to stay afloat.

The death of our dreams can be paralyzing. Matt told me he had killed his dreams. I was confused. According to him, he'd ruined his life. Matt started drinking in high school. Like all teenagers, he felt he would never become addicted. That happened only to other people. He knew the statistics, but he could never be one of them. He was seventeen. He was indestructible.

In college, Matt's drinking progressed. He experimented with drugs, but they had no appeal. He drank socially. Over time he married, had children, and started a business. Life was good. Only he knew that ten years later he would still need to have a drink before breakfast.

As the alcoholism progressed, Matt's life started to fall apart. His marriage disintegrated. His business went sour. His daughter stopped speaking to him. By the time he got to rehab, his life as he knew it was gone. After years of sobriety, he is still unable to forgive himself for his mistakes. Today Matt lives alone and distances himself from friends as he is afraid that in the end he will only hurt them too.

What happens when our dreams die? Langston Hughes asked in a "A Dream Deferred," Do you fester? Do you sag? Do you explode?

I THOUGHT THIS WAS WHAT I WANTED

For the majority, it was more subtle.

It seemed their plans had materialized. Their lives went as planned. They had decent jobs, good spouses, 2.5 kids, and a house—the whole package. And yet, they too said, "How come my life is not turning out like I wanted?" Their stories were not as dramatic, but they were equally painful. They had done what they had wanted to do but still felt something was missing.

These people, in some ways, were the most alone. They could not share their disappointments without sounding ungrateful; frankly, no one wants to hear about how hard a good life is. So when they came into my office, I understood that they were scared I too would judge them. But I knew that they came to me with fear, with desperation, and most of all with loneliness. They were searching for something but had no idea how or where to find it. They were looking for the answer but did not even know the question.

Jaime is "that" girl. You know, the one we all aspire to be. She has a ton of girlfriends, and the boys are in love with her. She is pretty and sexy. Cool and nice. Smart and savvy. Of course, she was destined to marry "that" guy, her mirror image. When she did, no one was surprised. He was partner at the law firm, a dog lover, a "hottie," rich, and from a great family to boot. Their romance was a whirlwind. Everybody fell in love with him as much as they had already fallen in love with her. In six months, they were engaged, and in a year, they were married. A few years later, you can imagine my surprise when we met for lunch one day and Jaime broke down. He is a workaholic. They never have sex. She pines for her high school boyfriend. And his mother calls daily to make sure he is properly fed. She got "everything," yet she feels empty.

For many of us, what we thought would make us feel complete doesn't. From early on, our world dictates to us a particular formula for success. And we believe it. However, the problem is that there is no one formula that works for everyone. If there was, we would live Stepford lives. For some people, having children is enough. For others it is enough only for a while. And for others it would never be right. The recipe for personal fulfillment is as unique as our DNA.

Each of these people got stuck. They lived completely different lives, but they shared suffering. It was not their intention to become inert; it just happened. By the time they got to me, they were resigned. But beforehand they had all shared a sense of shock and surprise. Things like this do not happen to me. My life was supposed to be different.

What was your life supposed to be like?

Ending the Excuses

Step Two

Everybody gets stuck at least once. Most of us get stuck a lot. Even though we are plenty smart—we know intellectually what the problem is, we may even know how to fix it—still we remain paralyzed. We give incredible advice to our friends. We tell them what they should do and how to change in order to live the life of their dreams. We even become annoyed and exasperated when they don't follow our guidance. It turns out they feel the same way about us.

In this step, you stop making excuses. You learn how to manage your fears. This step is a bridge between the world you want to leave and the world you want to enter. According to the Jewish tradition, the

world is a very narrow bridge and our task is not to
be afraid. Lucky for us, the bridge may be narrow
but it is not very high. You are not going to fall.

Don't be afraid. Walk on.

❧

Tenth-grade science taught me the principle of inertia. An object in motion stays in motion, an object at
rest stays at rest. People are no exception. We want
to change. But we can't. We have all kinds of excuses
and reasons we remain paralyzed and are unable to
move forward.

FEAR

The Israelites wandered the desert for forty years.
They could have made it in six. But their fear held
them back.

Standing at the threshold of the land of milk and
honey, Moses sent twelve of his most trusted leaders
to check it out. What are the people like who live

there? Would they make good neighbors? What is the food like? How is the weather?

The leaders had a mission to fulfill. They spent forty days exploring this new place. When they returned to give their report, their fears got the best of them. Even though the land was ideal, they described it as a place filled with giants and monsters. A place they could never live. Their fears became contagious. By the end of their stories, no one was willing to make the journey. It would be another thirty-four years before the Israelites would conquer their fears and enter the land.

Paralysis usually begins with fear.

Some fears help us stay safe. I want my son, Emet, to be afraid to cross the street alone. But I don't want that fear to engulf him and prevent him from ever crossing the street. While fear can be to our benefit at times, it can also overwhelm us, preventing us from living life fully.

In the Torah, God commands the people eighty-eight times to have no fear. He had to keep reminding them because their nature was to be afraid and to stay stagnant. Without God's urging, Noah would have lived forever in the ark. You would have thought the smell alone would have been enough to get him out. Moses, a man with a fear of public speaking, would have been too nervous to give us the Ten Commandments.

Fear is the opposite of faith. Fear is when we lack confidence in ourselves, in others, and in the world. Faith requires belief without always having logical proof. It is human nature to look for assurances. We seek them out. Before we go to a restaurant, we check Zagat, look at the online rating, and ask our friends. God forbid we should go in blind.

Sometimes our fears seem legitimate. We have responsibilities and obligations, and we use them as excuses not to make a change. My father never graduated from college. He always dreamed of going back to school. When we were children, he would remind us over and over again how it was impossible for him to fulfill his dream as he had bills to pay, kids to feed, and a mortgage.

What was he afraid of? He was afraid he would fail and disappoint himself. What if he was not the "smart" man he thought he was? If he did return to school and it was too hard, it would confirm his deepest fear, that he was a sham. He lacked faith in himself. It was easier for him to blame the circumstances than to face his fears.

Remember when you lined up the dominoes on the floor? One move and they all toppled. As adults, we are still playing. Only now we spend years lining up our lives in the same way. As mothers, as fathers, as employees, as adult children, we set up a delicate structure in which everything is relying on us. We believe that if we move one piece, the entire kingdom will collapse.

Many women talk to me about their need for a day off. They need a break. But they will not take one. How would their children get to school? Who would pack their lunches? Wouldn't their husbands resent their absence? How could they get time off work? How would the house stay clean? They are afraid that one day off will destroy the delicate balance that they have achieved over years of careful planning. Whenever I suggest a possible solution, they discount it. What they are really afraid of is that they are not as needed as they thought. They are afraid that a little time off will invalidate who they are.

What they do not know is that often their husbands talk to me as well. Their husbands want them to have a break. Their husbands know that they will be better mothers, wives, and people if they have time to nourish themselves. Often the people who love us need us

in different ways than we think. They need us to let
them care for us. They want to feel important as well.
When we are so afraid to let them, we do not validate
their roles in our life.

If fear prevents us from taking a day off, how much
more so from seeking a better future? The fear of
the unknown can be so debilitating that we refuse to
change our situation. We stay in mediocre relationships
because staying feels easier than leaving. What if there
is no next guy? What if this is the best I can do? What if I
am being too picky? What if I regret the decision? What
if he needs to age like a fine wine? What if it is me?

We stay stuck in our jobs and in our lives and ask
these questions again and again. We stay put because
we know what we are dealing with. Our fears imagine that the alternative will be worse, not better. Our
fears keep us from asking, "What if the next guy is my
soul mate?" "What if I do deserve better?" "What if I
prefer being alone to being partnered with the wrong
mate?" "What if I realize that I matter?"

Even though the Israelites were slaves in Egypt,
they were terrified to leave. Moses made them, but
even once they were out, they begged him to let them
return. Their fear of not knowing the future, where
they would live and how they would survive, made

slavery look tolerable. They pestered Moses with all kinds of questions. How much longer? When do we stop for food? Are we there yet? So it is ironic that once they'd arrived at their destination, their fears got the best of them yet again.

IF ONLY . . .

If only the good guys were not all gay.

If only I had more time, I would work out. If only I was smarter, funnier, thinner, richer, better looking, then my life would be perfect. Excuses often disguise themselves in the "If-only . . ." language.

Even now, as I am trying to write my first book, I say to myself, "If only I could retreat to a quiet cabin on a placid lake without kids, then I would be truly inspired." The logic is alluring because it is partly true. If I could buy a house on a lake, it *would* be quieter. But it would not mean that this book would be any easier. Writing takes time and effort. If I'd waited for that cabin, I would never have started, let alone finished. And it turns out that my rare moments of inspiration actually come from my kids.

We Plan, God Laughs

"If only . . ." is an excuse to keep us stuck. Everyone has a beautiful friend in a bad relationship. We all hear of lottery winners who end up worse off than before they won. We all know that the smartest person does not always get the promotion.

"If only . . ." is so easy because we are bombarded with images of people who appear to have better lives than we do. On any day it can seem like everyone else is more successful in every way. Unless we live on an island, it is inevitable that at some point we will compare and despair. Our mother mentions our sister's raise, and our eyes roll. Our coworker receives flowers from her husband, and we just know they have a better marriage than we do. Even the nameless woman in yoga seems more at peace than we are.

Standing in line for coffee, glancing at the covers of glossy magazines, we are reminded of how much less we have. We are not as beautiful as Salma, we do not have as much money as Warren, we are not as smart as Einstein. Not only do we have less than they do but we feel like we are less than they are. Surely, if we were deserving, things would be better for us. Every time we see another supermodel marry a rock star, hear the stories of our siblings' success or the genius of our neighbors' child, we become more afraid that we alone are not enough. Finally, one day, the doubts become so ingrained in us that we actually believe them. They pile on until we can no longer move.

In the *Inferno,* Dante describes the different levels of hell; the worst by far is at the center, where Lucifer dwells. Having been thrown out of heaven for arguing that human beings should not have free will, he finds himself frozen in ice, unable to move. He is truly physically paralyzed. Greek mythology echoes this notion that hell is being unable to move forward. Sisyphus pushes a boulder up a hill time and time again, never to reach the anticipated peak. Philosophers over the years have reminded us that it is not just uncomfortable to be stuck—rather, it is hell.

There are a million reasons why we stay stuck in the worst of all places, why we stay in a personal hell. It is far easier to make excuses. Starting the diet today is much harder than starting on Monday. But when Monday comes, it turns out the following Monday would be even easier. Now here we are. Mondays have come and gone, and we are still not a pound lighter.

Fill in the blank:
If only _____ *then I* _____ .

EXPECTATIONS

By thirty, are we supposed to have conquered the
world?

Ellen thought so. So at twenty-nine, on the verge
of becoming an "official" adult, she thought she was
already supposed to have published her first novel,
married an investment banker, traveled the world,
and gotten a Ph.D. Of course, she had finished none
of those things, and hysteria set in. She had only one
year to make it all happen. Just like cramming for college exams, she began cramming for life. She wrote
the first sentences of seven novels. She booked and
canceled tickets to travel all over the world. She col-
lected graduate school applications. She went on a
hundred blind dates. She kissed a lot of frogs. Her
thirtieth birthday came, and lo and behold, the world
did not end. Thirty was a number just like twenty-
nine. But she had expected it to be different.

We all have expectations. By thirty, we would be
financially successful. By forty, married with kids. By
sixty-five, retired. Except some of our expectations
along the way became illogical. We formed them
long ago, without any concept of the kind of person

we would become. We formed them without knowing the kind of life we would live and the people we
would and would not meet. Along the way, the expectations were reinforced by our parents, our teachers, and our society. No one meant to make us feel
bad. Except when we fell short of their expectations,
somehow we did.

> *What do you expect of yourself now?*

VEERING FROM THE PATH

We are all granted a few years to "find ourselves." Then
we are expected to get serious. We are expected to
stop wasting time. Real life starts now. So when I announced I was dropping out of rabbinical school in
the middle of my "real life" to backpack through Thailand, people reacted as though I had lost my marbles.

Before then, I was always living up to expectations.
I went to college. I was focused. So this announcement
took everyone by surprise. Some people just smiled
and nodded. But the ones closest to me showed their

disappointment. To them, it seemed like I was throwing away years of hard work.

I remember my father saying, "You are a smart girl. You are in graduate school heading toward a meaningful career. You have to go find yourself? What could you possibly find in Thailand that you cannot find here? In my day we could not just pick up and gallivant across the world." His sentiments were echoed by my peers and teachers. At the time, I was surprised by how many of them had wanted to travel off their paths but had not. They made me think that my dreams of exploring other cultures were frivolous. Was I just trying to avoid third-year exams?

It was not the first time that I had veered from the path. I was nineteen when I told my parents that I wanted to be a rabbi. They reacted as if I had told them I wanted to surf for a living. Up until then, I had heard only that they wanted me to be happy, so I expected, if not joy, at least their satisfaction that I had found out what my path was to be. But apparently they had been lying. The room was dead silent for what felt like hours, my parents just staring incredulously. Tears even came to my mother's eyes. When I finally mustered the courage to look directly at my father, the first words out of his mouth were "No. No, you are going to be a surgeon." Before I could answer, my mother put in her two cents. "Who is going to marry a girl rabbi?"

Their reaction struck a nerve. My parents know me better than anyone. At the time, I wondered if they knew me better than I knew myself. (Though I would never have admitted it to them.) Maybe life would be easier if I became a doctor. I spent a lot of time thinking about what they said. So much so that I started to wonder how much credence I should give their concerns. I wondered, Had their expectations become my own? Where did they end and I begin? I knew if I listened only to them, I would become a surgeon, ignoring my own true desires. If I discounted them completely, I would be acting like a rebellious child.

I had thought a lot about what my life would be like if I became a rabbi. At the time, there was little precedent for a woman who wanted to become a rabbi. In over five thousand years of Jewish history, there were maybe ten women Conservative rabbis. There was no set path. It was new to my parents. It was new to me. It was new to the world.

Was I ready to be a pioneer? What would religious people think of a reformer? Would people think I was a religious fanatic? Would I ever get a job? Would I be able to get married and have a life? Could I still wear a bikini at the beach?

WHAT DO YOU REALLY WANT?

Our own expectations can be just a tad unrealistic as well.

A forty-two-year-old single man, Joey, came to me to set him up. He said he wanted a nice Jewish girl. Someone who wanted a family. Someone his family and friends would love as well. Sounded doable. He was good looking, successful, personable. So, he lived with his mom. I could spin it that he was a devoted family man. "Anything else important I should know?" I asked. Without pausing, he said, "I want her to look like Brooke Shields." I laughed. He didn't. It turned out he was not joking. My list of possible matches was shrinking. Brooke Shields is six feet. At five four, I towered over most of my female congregants. I could work with the mom thing. But Brooke Shields? No wonder he was single. His inertia was not about the right woman. It was about his unrealistic expectations.

I find many people expected their lives to be extraordinary, yet they wind up feeling really ordinary. In our dreams, we are the best. We will not just be a doctor, we will cure cancer. We will not just be an entrepreneur, we will found the next Microsoft. We will not just have children, we will have children who are angels. Except in real life, getting into medical school is near impossible. Bill Gates would not even hire us. And the devil is no match for our children.

Or it may be that our expectations are just outdated. Our expectations are like vintage clothes. "Vintage" is most often a euphemism for "old and overvalued." We keep our old clothes in a closet thinking someday we will fit into them again or someday they will be back in style. We do the same with our expectations. We hold on to them far too long. And the longer we keep them, the less room there is for new possibilities.

At times our expectations become inflated into an ideal that can never be realized. Our fantasies sound reasonable at home on the couch. Watching a romantic movie with a bowl of popcorn, we begin to think that making love on the beach is the mark of true romance. How come your husband wants to have sex only at home? Does it mean that your marriage is just mediocre? When you finally drop enough hints, and he gets the message and you make the date, it is nothing like the movies. Who wants to leave her perfect outfit lying around in the sand? It is wet, sticky, and cold. It is the last place you want to make love.

When our expectations are too unrealistic, they become destructive not only to ourselves but to others as well. When a well-known radio personality asked me on a date, I thought I'd hit the jackpot. On air, he was adorable, charismatic, insightful, and funny. I was ready to plan our wedding and I had not even met him. When he came to the door, I was surprised to see a regular guy. He was not as cute as I'd expected. During dinner, we ended up spending a lot of time talking about the weather. By the end I knew there would be no second date. I never gave him a chance. I never let him leave the box that I had constructed for him. I doubt he really wanted to talk about the weather, but he could sense my lack of interest in who he really was. He knew I wanted Mr. Radio.

My expectations ruined a date, Elana's ended her marriage. Elana was raised in a privileged home. Her father had worked hard and become incredibly successful in finance, and she grew up with tremendous wealth. Her father was her icon. He came from nothing and built an empire. He was philanthropic and generous with everyone. She was young when she married a musician. He was talented and edgy. She had no doubt that he would become as big as Sting.

Fifteen years into the marriage, he was a successful studio musician. He loved his job, he made enough to send his kids to private school and own a home. But he was not a big name. He wasn't able to lend his name to prominent charities or build a second home in the Hamptons. Elana was disappointed by him, and he felt it. It turned out he was disappointed in her too. He thought that she would be the rock star's wife even after they had kids. She would want to go out after midnight to hear the latest band, sleep in until noon, and drink champagne in bed. Neither one of them could live up to each other's expectations. This situation became devastating and their marriage ended.

Expectations are complicated. It is hard to know how much to expect versus how much to accept. Usually, the higher the expectations, the more disappointed we feel. Every day I am learning the importance of accepting my husband, my mother, my children, my friends for who they are, not for who I think they should be. It can be hard. Some days I want them to be different. I am sure they feel the same way about me. But if I refuse to accept them as they are, I will destroy the relationships.

My family expected me to become a physician, get married, and take time off to raise a family. My community expected me to raise Jewish children. Those expectations weren't wrong. But they were not exactly right. I wanted to be a professional, and I wanted to have a family, but I did not want to have to pick one over the other. I did not want to be a spiritual leader just in my home. I wanted to be a spiritual leader.

Have you become so concerned with pleasing others and meeting their expectations that you have stopped hearing your own dreams? Have your own expectations become so entrenched that you have stopped honoring the people around you and your true self?

The commentary of the book of Leviticus teaches that in life you are given three names: One is the name that your mother and father give you. One is the name that other people call you. And the last one is the name that you make for yourself.

What name do you want to make for yourself?

III

GETTING PRESENT

STEP THREE

This is one of my favorite steps because you lose
weight without lifting a finger. In step three, you
drop off your baggage. Whether you are carrying a
designer suitcase or a tattered, weathered
carpetbag, you probably have back pain. When you
cease carrying so much unnecessary weight, it is
not just the physical pain that goes away. In this step
you discover your authentic self. You discover that
without all the junk, you can find a sense of calm
and serenity. You will learn to find acceptance in the
moment. This awareness will give you the strength
to move forward—not from a place of discord but
from a place of peace. Step three takes vigilance,

for as soon as you put down one piece of luggage, another one is lurking.

Go in peace.

❧

In life there are no "do overs." We all have a past.

At some point we all say "oops." We all have boys we wish we hadn't kissed. Classes that we could have done better in. Things we should not have said to our mothers. Turns we should not have made. We can ask ourselves, "Why did I spend three years dating that guy?" "Why did I stay in that job?" "Why did I take that advice so seriously when it did not feel right?"

We cannot erase time or go back. Things happened, but they are over. They no longer need to define us.

There needs to be a statute of limitations for blame, not only for blaming ourselves but for blaming others as well. My parents did not love me enough. They loved me too much. My father was married three times. My mother never hugged me. No one told me that I made them proud. My teacher told me I would amount to nothing. There was too much pressure on me. At a certain point, we have to stop the madness. Yes, your parents may have had a terrible marriage, your mother may never have hugged you, and you may have had a sadistic teacher, but only you can make it different now.

In the ninth century, Judaism developed an odd practice. Shortly before Yom Kippur, the day of repentance, Jews would swing a chicken above their heads three times reciting, "This is my exchange, my substitute, my atonement; this rooster (or hen) shall go to its death, but I shall go to a good, long life, and to peace." It was this bizarre act that enabled them to go on, and throw away all the baggage of the past year. It should be so simple. It is.

ASHAMAH

In Hebrew, "ashamah," the word for blame, also means guilt. Every time I walk into a Safeway market, I feel a twinge of ashamah. In third grade, I stole a caramel and got caught. We all laugh about it now, but I still remember it every time I step into any market. I can still picture not being able to look my mother and the manager in the eye as I apologized. To this day, I never sample from the bins. If I have a hard time letting go of a caramel, how much more so something that really matters.

Ashamah has a way of staying with us long after the event has passed. Blame and guilt originate from the same place. And it is only you who decides when they end. Both sentiments hold us hostage to our past. Until we let them go, they continue to hinder us.

I stopped talking to my father when I was in my twenties. I blamed him for hurting our family. I should have been relieved when my parents finally divorced, but I wasn't. My anger turned to rage, and I blamed yet another thing on my father.

After a while, my anger began to paralyze me. I was mired in guilt and blame, in ashamah. I felt guilty that I could not rescue my mother. I began to blame my father for everything: my temper, my overeating, my suspicion of the male species. In the beginning, feeling the anger was cathartic. It was healing. But then it became tiring. He was long gone, and I was still in the same place. He was starting a new life, and I was stuck in an old one. I was carrying ashamah with me everywhere. Being with me was no picnic. I brought my ashamah to classes, to my friends, even on dates.

Until one day I realized the ashamah had become

crushing. I did not want to live this way. I wanted to move forward. I wanted to value my learning, appreciate my friends, find love. I knew my father was never going to change. He was never going to ask for my forgiveness. He was not going to make amends to my mother. If I wanted to live my life, then I needed to make a decision—to let go of the ashamah without him.

It was not easy. My father was not necessarily worthy of forgiveness. I kept reminding myself I was not letting go for him. I was letting go for me. I was changing because I did not want to live in the shadow of anger all my life. Each morning I would imagine myself free from anger. Happy, peaceful, content. After a while, my imagined life became a realized one.

One day I called my father out of the blue. The conversation was stilted. He was expecting an irate, bitter daughter to yell at him on the phone. Instead I asked him how he was doing. I was not sure that I wanted a relationship with him, but I was not sure I wanted to live my life feeling resentful toward him. He was surprised. So was I.

> *Write down your oopses, ashamah, anger, and stolen cara-*
> *mels, pin them to a plastic chicken, swing it around your*
> *head, and toss the whole thing in the trash.*

GET OVER IT

I have gone through a lot of engagements. Fortunately,
only one was my own.

In rabbinical school, we learned how to officiate
weddings. I got an A in that class. So I figured that
weddings would be a piece of cake. I knew I would
meet with the couple a few times before the wedding
to discuss the ceremony, do the necessary spiritual
counseling, and answer any questions. I would come
to the ceremony on time, say some fitting words, fin-
ish within the requisite twenty-five minutes, and my
role would be fulfilled. Boy, was I wrong.

I quickly learned that being engaged is far more
than just planning a wedding. You would have thought
that by the time I got engaged I would know better.
Boy, was I so wrong. Again.

I got engaged the day before Thanksgiving, and by

the time the pumpkin pie was served, I was a wreck. Did my fiancé and I know each other well enough? Who would pay for the wedding? Would our parents get along? Where would we live? Could I be a wife? Would we become a statistic and divorce? Where was I going to find the perfect wedding dress? On top of my own angst, everyone had questions for me. Where and when are you getting married? Are you sure he is the one? Where are you registered? How big is the ring?

It turned out I was planning one of the biggest days of my life not only with Jeff but with three sets of parents, siblings, nieces, nephews, dozens of friends, and my whole congregation. And somehow I was also supposed to figure out how to partner with Jeff. Instead of feeling more connected to him, I ended up overanalyzing his every move. I barely remember the rehearsal dinner.

By the time couples come to their first meeting with me, they are so overwhelmed that they dream of eloping to Vegas. Getting engaged was nothing like they expected.

The bride was told that this should be the happiest time of her life. She may have fantasized about this day for years. Instead of being happy, she is not getting along with her future mother-in-law, her friends hate the bridesmaid dresses, and she is worried about the peanut allergies of her guests, half of whom she has never met.

In ancient times, marriage was not an agreement between two people; it was an agreement between two families. It was a full-fledged merger. It was not just that two people wanted to spend the rest of their lives together; it was the coming together of so much more. Not much has changed. It was complicated then, and it is complicated still.

Rocky engagements are normal. Being engaged is like sitting on the tarmac. You are not in the airport, and you are not in flight. And my task as their rabbi is to help couples get off the ground. From that day forward, I end up being not only their rabbi but also a part-time wedding planner, cheerleader, and therapist.

To get married, you have to get over a lot. Your parents may not become best friends with your in-laws. Every holiday will not be observed in the same way it was when you were growing up. Your husband may never agree with your shopping habits. While each of these things sounds minor alone, when thrown together, they add up. My job is to help the couple see that there are some things they need to let go of, some things they need to learn to accept, and some things they need to learn how to incorporate into their lives together, so that when they officially start their new lives, they are on the same page.

My husband had imagined living his whole life in Louisiana. As a rabbi, I knew there were very few opportunities for me there. We could not live in two states and be married. Compromising would have left us somewhere in the middle of New Mexico. One of us had to let go.

That was the beginning of a life of letting go. It does not matter where we are, Jeff will always watch the Final Four. I will never retire in an RV. We both had to learn how to incorporate each other's mothers if we wanted to form our own family. In order to move forward as a couple, we need to get over a lot.

Take three deep breaths: One . . . Two . . . Three.

This is what I say to the couple when they are finally standing before me under the wedding canopy, the chuppah. For the days and months leading up to their wedding, there has been a lot of planning, arguing, and forgiving. It would be easy for them to lose focus. "I hope I will not regret signing the prenup."

"Will my father and husband ever have a conversation about something other than sports?" "Did I remind the band not to sing 'Y.M.C.A.'?"

So I stop the bride and groom and remind them to become present.

I remind them because if they can be here now, they can be even stronger going forward. They will realize that the past happened. There were other boyfriends and girlfriends. That is part of what enabled them to appreciate each other and to fall in love. I remind them to let it go.

People ultimately get married because they want to grow. They want to change. They want to become better. They want to be more than what they are. And the wedding ceremony is that most celebrated time for people to begin this change.

Getting married is not the only way. Throughout our lives we have the desire to make changes. But we think we need to wait for a special event: the new year, a significant birthday, or even a tragedy. We never think that today, right now, could be the beginning of living the life we've dreamed of.

Today is perfect. This moment can be a new beginning. We think the day begins in the morning and ends at night. Your day can start again whenever you choose. Tomorrow is so far away. Let your new day begin now. Your new day starts when you decide that things are going to change.

> The Talmud teaches, "Act while you can." The Talmud understands that now is the most perfect time. Not tomorrow or the next day. This very moment.
> Look at your watch.
> This is the moment you will begin to change.

FORGIVENESS

Jacob was an identity thief.

He was Esau's baby brother, and as the oldest, Esau was supposed to receive the blessing of the firstborn, which meant he would inherit everything, even his father's love. Yet Jacob knew that without the cash and without the praise, his own chances of success were slim.

Esau had firstborn syndrome. When Isaac, his blind father, asked him to hunt game from the fields and make him a delicious dinner before he blessed him,

Esau left promptly. But Jacob was a mama's boy. So when his mother, Rebecca, saw that Esau had left, she and Jacob plotted to steal the blessing of the firstborn. Rebecca prepared a delicious stew for her husband. Meanwhile, Jacob covered himself in fur to imitate the hairiness of his brother. Then Jacob went to his father pretending to be the oldest son.

Isaac was fooled, and he gave Jacob the blessing. When Esau returned from the fields, he was steamed. Right there he vowed to kill his brother, Jacob. Jacob fled.

Years passed before Jacob saw Esau again. This time Esau had backup, four hundred men. Jacob knew his brother had not forgotten what he had done. He ran ahead, hoping that Esau would spare his family. Esau ran toward him. To Jacob's surprise, rather than strike him, Esau embraced his baby brother and kissed him. Then they wept in each other's arms.

Did Esau forgive Jacob?

Yes and no. If forgiveness means that he was okay with what happened, then no, he did not forgive him. But if forgiveness means that Esau was able to put the past in the past and move forward with his life, then yes, Esau did forgive Jacob.

Jacob never apologized to Esau. Maybe he did

not want to remind his older brother of his betrayal. Maybe he was a coward. Maybe he was too proud. Maybe he even thought he was right. His mother thought so. And Esau was no dummy. He remembered distinctly what had happened when they were boys. No one ever forgets the rivalry between brothers. Jacob did not deserve Esau's forgiveness.

Esau forgave in order to prevent the past from infecting the future. He knew that if he was weighted down by his history, he could never fulfill his real destiny as the father of Edom. This was a huge act of courage. After all, even with a shady past, Jacob ended up becoming a leader of Israel. Esau never planned on being his brother's new best friend. They did not hang out after this encounter. They reunited only once more, to bury their beloved father. But Esau needed to forgive Jacob.

We can hold on to resentments for a lifetime. We can spend hours, days, and months, even years, thinking about why things happened the way they did, why people said the things they did, why circumstances affected us the way they did. *Why* is a never-ending question. We can hold on to our resentments so tightly that letting go seems impossible. But we all know that if you make a fist, you can never hold on to anything else. The past is part of who you are, but it is not all of you. It happened.

Are you going to be an Esau and move forward?
Who will you forgive and who will you ask for forgiveness?

ANGER

You are a prophet.

A prophet (or prophetess) is a person who directly encounters God in some form. Judaism recognizes that each one of us is capable of prophecy. We all have the ability to communicate directly with God, without any intermediaries.

According to the Talmud, "Anger deprives a sage of his wisdom, a prophet of his vision." We can become imprisoned by our anger, anger that can seem so immense that it feels impossible to overcome. It is not.

One of the worst kinds of anger comes from tragedy, from circumstances that are impossible to explain or understand. No religion can give you answers or reasons for such events. But Judaism can give you frame-

works to move forward. One such framework is the
Jewish tradition of ritualizing the year of grief after
the loss of a loved one because we know that grief and
the anger that comes from it can be debilitating.

After a death, for the first seven days you wallow
in your grief, anger, and pain. You stay inside, sit on
low stools, and hibernate. Friends and family come
to visit and provide your meals. You are not even required to acknowledge their presence. You retreat entirely from society. At the end of that period, you get
up and walk around the block seven times, beginning
the second period of mourning. For the next twenty-
three days, you limit your interactions in the world.
You don't go to movies, but you may go grocery shopping. You do only what needs to be done. You slowly
begin to reenter society. From the end of thirty days
and continuing until one month before the anniversary of the death, you attend synagogue daily. You go
to work. You function in the world. However, you still
refrain from parties and celebrations. Right before
the anniversary of the death, you go to the cemetery,
you uncover the headstone, and you officially end the
period of mourning.

We can apply the mourning rituals to work through
all sorts of anger and grief. Instead of lashing out in

anger at everyone and everything around us, in the intensity of the moment we can retreat. We can find a place to feel truly angry instead of trying to fake it in that initial period. But that time is limited. Maximum stay is a week. Then it is time to find a place to reconnect. To begin to look at the situation, yourself, and others, and to discover where the anger actually belongs. Within a month, while the anger may not have passed, you must begin to push it aside, as hard as that is. Over the year, the anger becomes balanced with the rest of your life. By the anniversary, you realize that the anger is part of your life, not all of it.

Some anger may feel like it would take a thousand years to overcome. Don't let it. If the mourning of death is marked in a year, we can learn to move forward from almost anything in the same amount of time. At a certain point, we need to reconnect with the world. Even though it may not be the same world you left, you must engage once again. Spending a lifetime in anger prevents us from living now.

Don't think small resentments don't matter. When your friend loses your favorite earrings, your husband forgets your anniversary, your boss singles you out, you may not need a year to move forward, but you still have to make sure to put the anger in its proper place. You need to feel it, address it, and move on in order to be the prophet God wants you to be.

THE LABELS

High school reunions are weird.

There really is no better word to describe them. Twenty years pass, thirty years pass, even forty years. You have become a completely different person than you were in high school. But the minute you reunite with your classmates, it feels like you've been warped right back to that time and place all over again, and you once more feel trapped in the labels that defined you as a teen.

The labels of our childhood are insidious. They can continue to define us long into our adulthood and hinder us from moving forward.

Some of your labels may have been accurate at one time. You may have been a shy child. Some labels are societal. "Girls are not as good at math as boys." Some are constructive criticisms. "If you spent more time on homework, you would get better grades." Some were only passing comments. "You have childbearing hips." And some were just mean. "You would be so pretty if you cut your hair."

Whatever their origin, over the years, we have internalized those labels. They have become our truths. For as long as I can remember, my older brother was the smart one, I was the hard worker. I do not remember who first said it or why, but everyone knew. I always believed that I had to work hard to succeed. I could never rest on my laurels like my brother could. If I did, I would fail. It wasn't a terrible label. "Lazy" would have been worse. But at a certain point it was impossible for me to consider myself smart.

For my brother, it was the opposite. Everyone thought he was smart, so he was never allowed to fail. When he did not meet his potential, he was considered lazy. Twenty-five years later, we were sitting around the dinner table reflecting on our best and worst traits. As if he had never become a lawyer or started his own company, he immediately answered, "I am smart and lazy." It was as if we were fifteen all over again. In the same conversation, I described myself as "hardworking" and had to stop myself before I said, "Not so smart." As children, we had internalized the spoken and unspoken labels that were given to us. As adults, we are still letting them define us.

You might have been bookish, fat, intense, or nerdy. Or you might have been edgy, funny, athletic, or popular. But who are you now? Are you still holding on to a label that limits you? Are you still thinking that because you are pretty you can't be smart? Or because you are funny you can't be serious? As we age, we find we acquire even more labels. Now not only are we hardworking, but we are middle-aged, we are wives, we are mothers. Every label comes with even more limits. We could spend an entire lifetime living in our labels. Or we could determine that our labels are restrictive.

Today I've found that I can be both hardworking *and* smart.

Today you are given a page in a new yearbook.
Describe yourself as you are now.

THE SHOULDS

"Should" is a bad word.

When we say "I should have" over and over again, we drown out the more important words: "dream," "wish," "dare," "fulfill," "desire." "Should" silences our authentic selves.

Everyone has their shoulds. My brother should have gone to a better college. I should have been happy wherever I got in. I should go to law school. I should get married. I should stay home with my kids. I should send a thank-you note. I should wear a jacket outside. I should have dinner before dessert.

With the birth of each of our children, I continue to be in awe. They have the same father, same mother. I gained the exact same amount of weight with each pregnancy. They were even due the same week of different years. Yet they are entirely different. Everything about them is different: the way they look, what they eat, how they behave. I could "should" on them all day long. When I do, I am not honoring them as individuals. I am expecting them to fit into some generic mold.

It is time to shut off the "should valve." When you

hear yourself use "should" in a sentence, be wary. There is no present tense of the word "should." "You should" is in the future. "You should have" is in the past.

For you to be present, "should" needs to be eliminated from your vocabulary.

THE LISTS

Some people moonlight as bartenders. I moonlight as a matchmaker.

Most people think matchmakers are like the old woman in *Fiddler on the Roof*, but times, they are a-changing. Matchmaking is deeply rooted in the Jewish tradition. The Talmud even tries to push it as a career by saying that if you set up three couples who marry, you will be guaranteed a spot in heaven. Seems like a snap to get through the pearly gates. It is not.

People are not easy to set up. They tell me, "I want to get married," and then they pull out the list. For Joey, the perfect mate is between twenty-five and twenty-seven, is between the heights of five feet five and five feet seven, and has blue eyes. She must have attended an Ivy and played at least one musical instrument and one sport. Her parents must still be married. But only one quarter of the population has blue eyes, Ivy League acceptance rates are lower than ever, musical and athletic talents do not usually go hand in hand, and 50 percent of marriages end in divorce. Heaven is looking distant.

If I do check off the list and set two people up, the postgame commentary can be discouraging. "I would have liked her but . . . I can't date someone who doesn't read *The New York Times*, doesn't eat dessert, or has cats." The list gets longer. His heart did not race, her palms did not sweat, and there were no fireworks.

We all carry our lists. Whether you actually write them down or not, you have them. A list of what the perfect mate should be. A list of what you should do to be successful. A list of what should make you happy.

When we are checking our lives off a list, we restrict our possibilities. The love of your life may be five feet one with green eyes. She may never have attended college but still be the most interesting person you know. She may prefer *The Wall Street Journal* and be a diabetic. You may see stars only when you are dehydrated.

Let go.

Let go of lists, shoulds, labels, anger, blame, guilt, resentment.

Make a small change. When someone tries to take your parking space, drive away. When you see your backstabbing coworker, smile. When someone asks you your plan, don't begin your answer with "I should." Next time someone tries to set you up, just say yes. Take a small step and you will begin to move on. You have a choice. Move forward or stay put. Make the decision to move forward. Leave the past in the past.

Be here now.

IV

CELEBRATING THE
DIVINE YOU

STEP FOUR

Step four is a party—for *you*—without the hassle of
organizing invites, planning the food, and worrying
about what to wear. In this step, you learn how to
see the tremendous gifts you have been given. In life
we are trained to focus on the negative, to see what
we could do better rather than what we do well. We
only hear the one critic in a room filled with support.

This step teaches you how to see yourself differently.
How to see yourself the way God sees you. A
person who is divine. A person endowed with many
gifts. A person who deserves celebration. This
step is the best present you will ever give yourself.
Accept it graciously. Just say thank you.

༄

We Plan, God Laughs

I used to love my birthday. Don't we all at some point? Of course we do—a birthday is a celebration of us.

For months beforehand, my mom and I talked about the day and the party. Each one was carefully crafted, but I don't remember ever talking about my mom's birthday. I did not even know how old she was. I never understood why her birthday was not such a big deal. Until one day I did.

Starting from the day of our birth, we celebrate our potential. Birthdays are not about what you have accomplished or who you have become. Birthdays celebrate that you are here. You were born. You are in the world. With each year, your world grows and so does your excitement. At one, with your first steps, the world goes vertical. At sixteen, with a driver's license, your world becomes boundless. At eighteen, when you vote, you can change the world. By twenty-five, there is nothing you can't do.

Then one day you stop telling people your age. You stop celebrating. Birthdays no longer feel like celebrations of what awaits you; instead they mark what is past. Instead of feeling like the world is opening up in front of you, you feel like it is closing behind you. Suddenly, the future feels limited.

It is only a feeling.

Abraham Joshua Heschel, one of the most influential Jewish theologians of the twentieth century, was known for not only his scholarship but his commitment to civil rights and spirituality. He said, "The authentic individual is neither an end nor a beginning but a link between ages, both memory and expectation." At sixty you may have done a lot. You may have married, divorced, remarried, raised children, raised stepchildren, survived illness, changed jobs, traveled the world. But you are not done. You could never be done. There will always be more people to meet, places to visit, life to live. The possibilities in the world and inside of you are endless.

CELEBRATING YOU

Each month, Jews host a party for the moon.

The Jewish year is based on a lunar calendar, and every month we take note of the passage of time through the ritual of Birkat HaLevanah, the blessing and celebration of the new moon. What is surprising is when this ritual takes place. You would think we would celebrate the full moon, the night of romance. We don't.

Instead we celebrate when the moon is just a sliver in the sky and hardly noticeable. Most times we need a flashlight even to see the blessing on the page.

We bless the sliver because it expresses our faith in the future. We are blessing what the moon can become. It is a prayer of hope and belief and renewal. Though we know that each month the moon will wax and wane, the real purpose of this ceremony is to remind us that we are like the moon. We can become new again. We can uncover more potential and find even more of our beauty. As it says in the prayer, "Blessed are you, God, who says to the moon each month, you will be new again just like my children."

Your potential is unlimited. Each day, God revels in you. From the day you were born until the day you die, God is celebrating you.

God is not celebrating how much money you have made. God is not celebrating your job title or your house. God is celebrating each day that you are in his world. Each day you have the potential to imitate him: to create, to better, to discover, to build, to repair, and to laugh. That is God's party, a joyous celebration of each one of his creatures discovering her or his divine purpose.

God does not stop celebrating when you are thirteen, fifty-three, or even ninety-three. Just like my mom never stopped celebrating my birthday. She still makes it a big deal, even now. We are God's children. Just like we celebrate our children and see all that they can become. God thinks that our best selves are always in front of us. Whether it is your second birthday or your seventy-second, God is hoping you will discover more about your incredible soul with each passing year.

See Yourself Like God Sees You

"Show me who you are." This is a challenge that even God had to answer.

Moses needed to know. God could have shown his face to Moses. God could have told Moses about all he had done in creating the world. God could have refused Moses' request.

Instead, God used thirteen attributes to describe himself. When translated into English, they can be summed up by the following ten: compassionate, gracious, slow to anger, truthful, faithful, abounding in kindness, merciful, and forgiving of iniquity, transgression, and sin.

With this description, you would never think that this is the same God who destroyed Sodom and Gomorrah or caused the flood that ended the first world. But this is the way God sees himself. God sees what he can become.

Can we see ourselves the same way?

As part of my once-upon-a-time expectations, I always imagined I would meet my future husband after everything was in place. When I was established in my career, had worked out my issues with my parents, and had everything together. When I saw Jeff from across the room, I did not think he would notice me. I thought he would see what I saw, a girl in transition. I had just moved to Los Angeles. I was new in my career. And by Hollywood standards, I was definitely chubby. I never imagined he would approach. He did.

Later he told me that the day we met, I sparkled. I laughed and told him it was my glittery eye shadow. But we both knew it wasn't. When we met, we both sparkled. We saw in each other possibilities. We saw in ourselves potential. We saw what God saw.

God wants us to see ourselves in the same way God sees us. What are your thirteen attributes? Look within.

Whether they are big or small, they all matter. If you have had the same friends your entire life, you are clearly loyal. But you are also forgiving and patient. You are a person who embraces others' growth. To glean all this just from the fact that you like to hang out with your friends from grade school is not just a way to pat yourself on the back. It is not an act of arrogance. It is an act of God.

If you once said about yourself that you cannot have a relationship because you have commitment issues, realize that you are a loving friend, which might just translate into being a great boyfriend or even spouse. Don't say, "I can't cook, therefore I am not a good mother." Instead say, "I am a great mother. I can tell bedtime stories like no one else."

Diamonds and coal both come from the same substance, carbon. Though you probably never want to wear a coal ring, they both ultimately do the same thing, sparkle: diamonds when they catch the light, coal when we light it. Whether you see yourself like a diamond or like coal, with your thirteen attributes, you can transform into a ray of divine light.

Identify your thirteen attributes.

REVELATION

What does "revelation" mean?

Revelation is one of those words that is thrown around in religious circles, and no one knows what the heck it means. It sounds huge. Some people think revelation was when God gave Moses the Ten Commandments on Mount Sinai. But the Kabbalists, the believers in the Jewish mystical tradition, define revelation as "an act of self-disclosure."

According to that understanding, revelation occurs every day. Every time you uncover a new aspect of yourself, it is a revelation. When God told Moses about himself, that was God's revelation. When you discover more about your divine self, that is your revelation. Revelation never ends, for we are always in process.

I never expected that five fourteen-year-old girls would help me deeply understand this important lesson. Each week, the teenagers met with me to talk about growing up Jewish. We would discuss everything from cheating in school to attending weekly worship. One of the girls' mothers was dying of brain cancer, and each week, this girl would share her pain with the group. With her consent, I suggested to the girls that we visit her mother. At first they demurred. They had all kinds of excuses. "She won't want us to see her." "My parents don't want me to go." "I have too much homework." It took a while to break through. But finally the day came.

When we rang the doorbell, I was not sure what to expect. How would these teens comfort someone so ill? Would they be frightened when they saw her? Would they fall silent? Would they say something inappropriate? Out of nervousness, would they get the giggles? We had prepared for this moment, but would our preparation matter?

We went inside. We made a circle around the mother's bed. We clasped our hands, and together we began to pray. I started, but soon the girls took the lead. We had practiced this ritual, but I had never seen them take control. I was in awe. They were discovering something about themselves that they had never seen before. They had the ability to comfort, to heal, to care for someone that they did not even know. It was a revelatory moment for me and for them.

Since that time I have seen people of all ages discover in themselves qualities that they never knew they possessed. One man who was married for forty-five years told me that, after his wife died, he could never love again. He thought he was done. There was no more love to give. Yet when he met Estelle, at age eighty-four, he discovered that there is always more. Each day reveals more about love, Estelle, and himself.

Sometimes revelation can be confused with reinvention. When we think of the act of invention, we think of something artificial. When we think of the act of revelation, we think of discovering something real. We are seeing something that was already present in the world. We just did not know about it before.

Within you is a God-given, magnificent soul that has the potential to grow exponentially if you dare to let it. You have extraordinary qualities, more than you may expect—qualities that will be your tools to help you live the life you dream.

Imitateo dei. Imitate God.

Just like God, define your best self.

Discover your potential. Reveal all that you can become.

Have a party with the friends who treat you like a diamond. Put thirteen candles on the cake and celebrate the divine you.

PARTNERING WITH GOD

STEP FIVE

In Judaism you always study with a partner, a
havruta. This Hebrew word (meaning "fellowship")
is derived from the word for friend. The assumption
is that only when we are partnered with a friend can
we truly understand. In step five, we find our ideal
partner. We find that, on the route to our divine life,
we are not alone.

In this step we find encouragement and even
comfort. For some of us it may be surprising. Up to
now you may have believed this was a solo journey.
But all along, you have had a havruta, and in this
step you discover how powerful that can be.

∾

Whether you are a believer, a nonbeliever, or an agnostic, God matters.

The fact is that 90 percent of the people in the world subscribe to the idea of something greater than themselves. The concept of something greater than us exists powerfully in our world for a reason—because together, you and God have more power than you think.

God, Allah, Mother Nature, Beauty, Truth. The Hebrew Bible refers to God by seventy different names. Most of us read the Bible in English translation, in which God is called G-o-d. But in the original, God is referred to in multiple ways. Some are more popular, like Yahweh and the Lord; some are not, like El Shaddai, El Roi, and Elohim. When Hagar spoke to God, she called him El Roi, "the God who sees me." She named him such because he saw her deepest suffering, the suffering that others could not see. At other times God is called El Shaddai, "the God who says, 'Enough!,'" the God who is tired of his people acting like babies. The Bible is telling us that God's name changes as frequently as our relationship with God changes.

WHO IS IN CONTROL?

Call God whatever you want.

Just know somehow that God is in your life. But to what degree? Are we the passengers and God is the driver? Is God the passenger and we are the drivers?

Let's say God is in control. God is Mario Andretti, and we are just along for the ride. This God may sound familiar. This was the God I was taught about as a child, the old man with the long, gray beard, who sits on a throne in judgment. With this God, our actions are relatively meaningless, because this God has a master plan for each and every one of us. What we do and what we say is dictated by him. We are his puppets, and he is the puppeteer.

This God does not care about my suffering and pain. He is too removed. Too busy. My pain is part of his bigger plan. When I suffer, there is a reason, but I may never know it. Perhaps I am supposed to learn some lesson. But how do I know when I have learned what God is trying to teach? Does he keep testing me until I do?

When my father was diagnosed at fifty-eight years old with pancreatic cancer, the prognosis was terminal. I did not want to believe it at first. The year before he had gone to Africa to climb Mount Kilimanjaro. He looked healthy, and he had so much more life to live. For the first few months, he seemed just fine, so it was easy for me to deny the impending reality. I thought somehow he would be the exception to the rule. Until the disease began to take hold.

One night in the ICU, as my father was vomiting blood, I spoke to God directly. "Did you make him sick on purpose? Are you punishing him for the abuse? What can he do to repair the damage? If he did repent, would you grant him a few more months, a few more years, even a healthy future?"

These questions made me stop and think. Did I deserve this too? Was I fated to watch my father suffer a painful death because of something I had or had not done? In my twenties, I had stopped speaking to my father. Was this God's way of getting back at me— making it so that I would never be able to talk to my father again?

I could not stop obsessing. I had made plenty of my own mistakes. Would I too deserve this kind of punishment? What would my punishment be? When would God inflict it? Was there anything I could do to prevent it? If there was, would it be enough?

This God was keeping me up at night worse than any horror movie. He was scary in the worst kind of way.

I started to think maybe this was a test. Maybe God was grading me. But I wanted answers, not more questions. I wanted to know how to pass. Believing it was a test for even a moment made me hate God. I wanted to scream at him in a time that I needed him most. The last thing I needed in my pain was another lesson. Believing in a God who has a master plan would have meant that God had planned that my father would die before he could even meet his grandchildren.

A few days before my father died, I remember staring at this older couple on a park bench. Why did they get to live a long life? Did God like them better? Was my father not necessary to God's plan? Was he less important? I had to fire this God.

But if God was no longer employed, was I the boss? If I was in charge, then what was God doing? Was God just observing my father suffer? Watching my brother and me weep as he died before us? Was God tuning in to my life the way I tune in to a soap opera—*The Days of the Life of Sherre Hirsch*? Did God have no empathy for the characters?

Even worse was the idea that God and I were not

connected at all. This meant that I was utterly alone in this world. My actions here on earth did not matter one bit. God did not care because he did not know me. I did not even figure into this God's plan.

A powerless or indifferent God was just as problematic as an all-powerful one. I knew I needed something different. A God who could be far greater than I but at the same time care deeply for me. A God who could weep with me, rejoice with me, even laugh with me.

A NEW GOD

The first time I read that God may not be all-powerful, I was fifteen. I did not believe it.

It was not until years later, when I reread *Why Bad Things Happen to Good People* by Rabbi Harold Kushner, that I realized it could be true. I was floored. God might not have control? God may not intervene in our affairs and in the universe? All the evils of the world were not God's fault? God might be off the hook!

I realized that I needed a caring God far more than I needed an all-powerful one. I needed a God who comforted me through the pain more than I needed a God who caused it. Ultimately I came to believe that my God could be both limited and infinite. He could have an infinite capacity of create but no ability to control. He could have an infinite capacity to empathize but no ability to intervene. My God could not force anything to happen, but at the same time he would always be with me. My God has infinite compassion for each one of us individually. My God cares for me and for you.

Thomas Jay Oord, a contemporary Christian theologian, is one among many who argues that out of love and out of the desire to have a relationship with us, God gives us free will. God exchanges his control over us in order to have a partnership with us.

From the very beginning of creation, human beings were working with God to establish the world. By day six, God and humans were already working toward a partnership. As in all relationships, as the dynamic between us and God grows, we are both changed. God is affected by us just as much as we are affected by him. We are strengthened by each other. What we could do together is far greater than what we could do alone.

The Jewish tradition teaches that "whatever was created during the six days of creation needs further doing: Mustard needs sweetening, lupines need sweetening, wheat needs grinding, even man needs finishing."

Abram a.k.a. Abraham was ninety-nine years old when God established that the two of them would form a covenant, a partnership. From early on, God knew that together they would be more powerful than apart. Instead of sealing the deal in spit or blood, God gave Abraham the letter from one of his names, YHWH. With that letter Abram officially became Abraham, and their destinies were forever intertwined.

This is the ideal partnership. Without Abraham, God had no one to father the people. He needed Abraham. So too Abraham needed God. Without God, Abraham would never have had the support to leave his home. He would have been living with his idol-worshiping father into his hundreds.

God gave Abraham plenty of potential. But without the urging of God, the knowledge that God was on his team, Abraham may never have lived up to it. He may never have discovered his capacity to change his circumstances. He may never have realized that he did not have to stay stuck. He had the power to embark on a new adventure.

God gives each one of us our own music, but we write the lyrics.

You may not consider yourself a musician. You may feel safe singing only in the shower. You may even think you are completely tone-deaf. But you have soul. God gave it to you. It is the heart of your song, but only you can make it a hit. With your lyrics, you can soar to the top of the charts.

God has the mega iPod and values Marvin Gaye, Eminem, and Bach. God wants all the songs of his creations. He loves music. God knows that some of us will make pop, some will make R & B, some will make classical, and some will make something altogether different. He wants to hear all of it. Eleanor Powell, a movie star and dancer of the thirties, said, "What we are is God's gift to us. What we become is our gift to God."

Sometimes if there were words alone, the music would be flat. Sometimes if there were notes alone, the music would be discordant. With words and notes together, there will be masterpieces. We have far greater abilities when we combine God's gifts with our own. God gives us grapes, we make wine. God gives us wheat, we make bread. God gives us trees, we make homes. God gives us water, we make Diet Coke.

That is the definition of a true partner. In less technical terms, God is your personal trainer. Your favorite teacher. God is your spouse. God sees your beauty, your talent, your potential. God is the yin to your yang. God is the peanut butter to your jelly. God completes you.

An Ideal Partner

Each life will have a beginning, a middle, and an end.

At the beginning, God is in front. He gives each one of us unique tools and talents. Then he lets go and steps back—not behind us but beside us. He is always right there next to us.

God walked next to Enoch. Who? Enoch is mentioned for the first and only time during the "begets." You know, the genealogical part of the Bible, which we all ignore. Enoch seems like a nobody. What we know about him from the original text is that he was born, he bore children, and then he died. The one other thing we know about him is that he "walked with God." At first Enoch's mention seems superfluous, but the Bible is telling us if a regular guy like Enoch can walk with God, so can we.

It came as a surprise to my congregants that I was just like Enoch—regular. My congregants expected me to be a rabbi with a capital R. They expected that I was a pious, serious soul who contemplated life's deepest questions. They were surprised enough that I was a woman. But a former cheerleader? They expected their rabbi to have a direct line to God, a special "in" with the big guy, and somehow cheerleading did not fit into that picture. But cheerleading taught me how to root for others. It is not that different from what God does for us. God cheers. God cheers for us to overcome the odds. Become our best selves. Realize our goals. Just like the football players knew that they played best with the cheerleaders' support, we play best with God's support.

God says "You can" when you say "I can't." God asks "Why not?" when you ask "Why?" This is God's way. God has been doing it since day one. When God first appeared to Moses at the burning bush and commanded him to go to Pharaoh and free the Israelites from Egypt, Moses balked. Moses, the man with the direct connection, the very definition of a leader, said, "Who am I?" He did not feel qualified for the job. He was panicked. He had a speech impediment. He was supposed to lead the people? But God knew better.

He responded without hesitation, "I will be with you." God wanted Moses to know that, even when Moses doubted himself, God did not doubt him. God was not going to physically lead the people, but he would be with Moses for the ride.

Sure, God's relationship with Moses seemed exceptional because Moses was talking to a fireproof bush. But it wasn't. Moses was regular. He stuttered. He felt fear and self-doubt. He was one of us. Our relationship with God can mirror his. For God says to each one of us, "I am with you."

God wants each one of us to shine. In his solar system, each one of us can be a brilliant star. Although Moses' light was more famous, it was no brighter than anyone else's. We know that God does not show preferential treatment because when God described his people to Abraham, he did not highlight any one particular person. He said, "My people will be as numerous as the stars in the sky." God cares for our individual radiance. Without the light of each one of us, the world would be dark.

VI

RE-CREATING YOUR
CREATOR

STEP SIX

At the end of the sixth day, when God was
exhausted and ready to take a break, he took one
last moment to create humankind.

In this step you learn how to continue the creation
that God began. The goal of this step is to discover a
God with whom you can truly communicate. A God
who listens when you speak, and a God you listen to
when he speaks. A God who can help you live your
divine path. But in order to know that God, you
first need to discover him.

This does not mean that you have to start over
with God. It does not even mean that you have to
begin with God. But this step gives you the tools to

re-create a relationship that works for you. One in which you want to further the task that God began with you.

&

Maybe just the word "God" conjures up a particular image for you.

Maybe your God looks the way Michelangelo painted him in the Sistine Chapel. An old man with a long white beard and glaring eyes, pointing down at you. Maybe there are some slight variations. He sits on a throne. He has a scepter. He has blue eyes, not brown. Maybe he is a she. This guy does not know you. He is far away and very, very high up. How could anyone possibly partner with this God?

When I was a child, my parents forced me—and I mean forced—to go to Hebrew School. Two hours every Tuesday and Thursday, and three hours on Sunday, I sat in a classroom chanting Hebrew songs, learning Hebrew letters, and studying the Jewish holidays. My non-Jewish classmates suffered the same fate, only theirs had a different name. My teachers were Israelis; theirs were nuns. But we commiserated together. Mostly we were expected to learn by rote. Repeating words, prayers, even other people's ideas. On occasion we talked theology and philosophy, but even that was not a discussion, it was an oration.

The first time I challenged the notion that God was an old man with a white beard sitting on a throne, I was immediately sent to the principal's office. I was fortunate; my parents were pleased with my audacity. That reprimand led to years of exploration. Most of my friends learned a different lesson. Do not challenge the authority. If your teachers and your parents say "don't ask," then don't ask. But the minute you stop asking about God, God gets stuck. We matured—our minds, our bodies, our emotions—but God and our theology froze in time. We had become adults, but God had not grown with us. We were still talking to the third-grade God. Who can find a compatible partner in a third-grader?

It is time to re-create your creator. Doing so may feel daunting. You may have lived so long with your antiquated image of God that it seems impossible to create a new one. But God is waiting to be rediscovered.

God wants you to know him even better than you know your best friend. God wants you to create the partner in him that you can relate to. God wants you to see all of him. God does not want to be limited to one image from a painting that belongs to one painter.

What would your God look like? Is your God a babe? Would he be young or old? Thin or chubby? Tall or short? Human or element? Feeling or thought?

What would your God feel like? Would he be soft or prickly? Coarse or smooth? Gentle or gruff?

What would your God sound like? Would he sound like the waves or the birds? The country or the city? The breeze or the tornado?

Would your God have a personality? Would it be wise or sharp? Serious or sentimental? Humble or arrogant? Apologetic or proud?

Too Many Rules

Looks are not enough.

This is the reason you did not necessarily marry the best-looking guy you ever saw. You ended up with the guy you talked with for hours on the phone. The one you connected with. To really know another, it takes more than one date. It takes communication. Now you have a beginning with God. You have a place to start a new relationship.

To really connect with your God, you've got to start talking.

Each one of us is entitled to talk to God, but we don't always believe it. We think that because people are starving in Africa, dying in South Central, we do not deserve to be heard. We were taught certain unbreakable rules: "ice cream is not a meal," "say thank you," "never pray for yourself." Before sleep, kneel at your bed, clasp your hands, and ask God for health and happiness for your family and friends. This is what the good kids did. They never asked for a bicycle or a dog.

At church or at synagogue, there are even more rules. Dress appropriately, sit quietly, stand when you are told, repeat on command. It did not matter what you thought or how you felt as long as you did it "right."

When I was a kid, every holiday started the same way: my mother yelling at my brother about what he was wearing, with him yelling back at her, "God does not care if I wear jeans." My mother responding, "I could care less what God thinks; at synagogue no one wears jeans."

This was just the beginning. When we found our seats, the rabbi became our air-traffic controller. With just a gesture of his hands, we knew when it was time to rise. As long as I was mouthing the words, I could hide my Judy Blume books in the pages of the prayer book. My friend was even more clever; he simply repeated "elephant, elephant, elephant," so he actually looked like he knew what he was doing.

Even with all the pomp and circumstance in the sanctuary, there were moments that I talked to God. In synagogue when I spoke to God, I asked him to help the children starving in Africa and stop the Cold War. But I never would have spoken to him about something personal in "His House."

There were too many rules. I wanted to talk to God about the most serious crisis and the most mundane matter. I wanted to tell God about my despair over eating a pint of Ben & Jerry's. I wanted God to be as ecstatic as I was when I lost five pounds.

I soon figured out that synagogue was where I hung out with my friends; my bedroom closet was where I talked to God. It was there that I told God about my period, my parents, and my crush on Shaun Cassidy. In that space, God did not care about how I was dressed or what page I was on.

That was the beginning of how I learned to talk to my God. As I got older, the conversation grew and we had even more to talk about. "Where were you in the Holocaust?" "Do you even exist?" "Why do people divorce?" "Why am I getting a C in Astronomy?" As in all relationships, we had our ups and downs. Sometimes I would be so annoyed, I would stay silent for weeks. Other times I was Chatty Cathy.

Today I find myself back in the bedroom closet praying each night. With more kids than rooms in our house, my newborn daughter sleeps there, and every night our entire clan squishes in to pray with her before bed.

SPEAKING YOUR OWN LANGUAGE

Every teacher says there are no stupid questions. But nobody really believes that.

So when a rabbinic student asked Abraham Joshua Heschel, "How come sometimes when I pray, the spirit doesn't move me?" his classmates laughed. AJH was no regular teacher, and they were all star pupils, intellectuals. They waited for him to slam the student for asking something so emotional. They waited because they were sure this was the stupidest question that had ever been asked of this awesome scholar.

Instead, in the great Jewish tradition of answering a question with another question, Heschel paused and smiled. "My son, did it ever occur to you to try and move the Spirit?"

Find your own language to talk to God. You can speak in eloquent and poetic words, or you can just cut to the chase. You can sing, whisper, cry, scream, or laugh. You can talk by yourself, with others, at the beach, in yoga, in traffic, in a restaurant, even in the shower. God talked to Moses at Mount Sinai because it was the smallest, the least significant, of all the mountains.

Language is personal. The Buddhists talk in silence, the Hasidim in noise. If you are in Jerusalem, you might leave a note in the Western Wall. And yes, you can even talk to God in church or synagogue. God hears you everywhere.

In the first book of Samuel, we learn that Hannah was desperate for a child. She did not know where to turn or what to do; she had followed all the rituals and customs and said all the right prayers. In complete frustration, she went to the Temple. Rather than go inside, she stopped at the entrance and began to weep uncontrollably. She began to bargain with God. She vowed that if God gave her a child, she would dedicate that child to God. She was so engrossed in her pleas that she did not even notice the priest, Eli, watching. What he saw was Hannah crying and mumbling half-crazed words. He thought she must be drunk because her lips were moving but he did not hear anything intelligible. Yet God heard everything.

By all typical standards, Hannah did everything wrong. Instead of making the traditional offerings to God through animal sacrifice, she offered her soul. Instead of entering the Temple, she stood outside. Instead of praising and applauding God, she told him of her unhappiness and her despair. Instead of asking for others, she asked for herself. She gave God her heart.

You might not use words. The Baal Shem Tov, the Jewish mystic and rabbi who founded the Hasidic Jewish movement, said, "In all your ways know him." We can talk to God with our tears, our laughter, our passion, our minds. You might meditate, dance, swim, walk. When Abraham Joshua Heschel marched with Martin Luther King, Jr., he said that his "legs were praying." A member of my congregation told me that she spoke to God with the birth of her first child.

We Plan, God Laughs

Whatever language you use when you re-create your creator, there is only one rule: Converse in a language you understand. The Shulkhan Arukh, the definitive legal guide for modern Jews, stipulates that we must pray in a language we understand. If your childhood rituals still leave you feeling empty, start with the words of the Rambam, one of the most pre-eminent medieval Jewish theologians: "Speak your heart." Let your heart be your guide. Develop the words and rituals that move your soul.

We all know the cliché "The journey of a thousand miles begins with the first step," i.e., the diet starts with the first grapefruit. The relationship begins with the first hello. Once you get past the small talk, the conversation starts. Eventually you develop a shared language. My husband and I can share a look across a table and know exactly what each other is thinking. So too with God; over time you develop your own private lingo.

With this God, there is no need to edit. There is no proofreading, spell-checking, or deleting. It is a relationship you cannot have with anyone else. With your spouse you claim there are no secrets. But you wouldn't repeat something that would hurt his feelings. And does he really need to know about every new pair of shoes? You never have to worry about hurting God's feelings. God already noticed your shoes.

So chat with abandon. Talk away. Tell God everything.

God is accessible 24/7. No need to make an appointment on your BlackBerry. You don't have to squeeze him in between meetings. You don't need to "do lunch." The Kotzker Rebbe, a famous Hasidic rabbi, said that "God dwells wherever we let God in." Abraham worshiped at Mount Moriah. The Israelites prayed on the journey through the desert. Jesus was homeless when he preached the gospel.

Now that your God may be as wise as Gandhi, as selfless as Mother Teresa, as charismatic as Martin Luther King, Jr., as good-looking as James Bond, with sprinkles of Dear Abby, Dr. Ruth, and your favorite teacher, you are ready to listen, to hear what God is saying to you.

A friend is listening: let me hear your voice.
—Song of Songs 8:13
Be experimental: The next time you talk with God, sit instead of stand. Shout instead of whisper. Go outside. Do something differently.

VII

FINDING YOUR
DIVINE SPARK

STEP SEVEN

In step seven, we learn that the world was created
for each one of us individually. We discover that we
were born with divine sparks, and our task is to
bring them to the world in which we live. It turns
out these sparks have been with us all along. We just
were not paying attention.

In step seven we pause and listen to what God has
been telling us all our lives. Our spark is unique.
Our spark is valuable. We are important to God and
to the world. Once we learn this about ourselves,
we can fan our sparks into a flame.

Listen. Sh'ma.

The Jewish credo is a short prayer named after its first word, "listen." Jews are commanded to say it four times a day. Perhaps we are not such good listeners. Listening is hard. When people talk, we often tune them out, whether they are our boyfriends, our buddies, our bosses, our bubbies.

Listening to God is even harder. At least with people, when their mouths are moving, we know they are speaking. With God, it is entirely unclear. In the movies, when God speaks, it is dramatic. The waters part, the waves tremble, the earth shakes, and the voice of God booms. In life, the drama is not there. It is far more subtle. Often God speaks to us in the stillness and quiet. Elijah heard God in a still small voice. Likewise, the way God speaks to us may not be loud and intrusive but rather quiet and intimate. Moses asked to see God "face-to-face" so he could speak directly to him. God refused. Moses really had to learn the art of listening. So do we.

Listen.

God is telling you something extraordinary. You are made in God's image, and you are entirely unique. You are the only you in the world. Even if you are an identical twin, you and your twin are not the same in every way. Each one of us is a creation of God. It is not that we share physical similarities or similar tastes. We share an element of the divine.

The Hasidim believe that God endows each one of us with a divine spark. It radiates from within us. Our task in life is to discover that spark and turn it into a flame.

If you are anything like me, most days you do not wake up feeling sparkly. I wake up sleep deprived, to demanding children and a long to-do list in my head. I find my way to the bathroom to begin the routine: toilet, teeth, face. My day starts in an exceptionally regular way. Taking a shower, making coffee, or being drained by my two-year-old's tantrum don't make me feel like I am special.

But in the Jewish tradition, every moment of our lives is singular. From the moment we wake, we are commanded to transform these mundane moments into divine ones. We blink, we bend, we pee, and after each one we say a blessing. Yes, there is even a blessing after you go to the bathroom. When I teach this to preteens, I am always met with peals of laughter. The rabbis did not command us to say these blessings to make us feel silly, nor were they intending to make us spend the day repeating endless words of gratitude.

They wanted us to elevate a life of routine into a life of holiness. To remind each one of us that, while we may feel tremendously regular when we wake, we are anything but. We are creations of God. We sparkle.

You may not believe it at first. But by reminding yourself again and again, you will come to know it is true. It is like the first day working out; you do not feel motivated, let alone thinner. But day after day, the routine becomes easier, the motivation increases, and lo and behold, you cannot imagine life before working out.

Your sparkle will not come from a sequined dress. You will not wake up one day showered in light, surrounded by angels, feeling divinely inspired. It will be much more subtle. After a while you will just know. You have a divine spark unique to you that the world is waiting to see.

BABY, YOU SPARKLE

So what is your spark?

Remember a time that you felt everything was right. The world just worked. You were in the moment. You felt alive, calm, complete. There was no other place you wanted to be but right there. Everything about that moment worked. It could have been a short moment. It could have been when you were a child. It could have been with a friend, with family, with a stranger, or when you were alone. It could have been in a time of transition or doing something you have done for years. It does not have to be a star moment when you won an award or got the lead in the play. It does not even have to be a moment that anyone else recognized. Whenever you felt it, for some reason it has been enduring. The moment has stayed with you.

In Judaism, we call this moment "shleimut." The root of the word comes from "shalom," peace. At every juncture we felt shleimut, our divine spark was ignited. You may not have realized that all those moments contained the essence of your deeper truth. But they started early on.

In seventh grade, I ran for class president. I remember my first speech to the sixty tweens in front of me. I was nervous. At thirteen, you peers matter. But I walked up to the podium and I took a deep breath. I stumbled at first, but then I felt a sense of calm come over me. I looked up into the faces of my classmates and I knew I was exactly where I was supposed to be.

We Plan, God Laughs

When I remember that moment and the ones that
followed, I see that there has been a consistent theme.
In college, I was passionate about fund-raising for Israel. In Kappa Kappa Gamma, a non-Jewish soror-
ity, Israel was not a top priority. When I gathered my
"sisters" for a meeting to share my passion and commitment, as soon as I began, I had another moment.
I have had many. Helping my younger neighbor with
her homework. Teaching Melissa and Brandy how to
play tennis. In all of those moments, I was communicating.

I have always been told that I have the gift of the
gab. Usually it worked against me. I was sent to the
principal's office for passing notes, talking too much,
disrupting the class. I always liked to talk. Not all my
speech was divine. Words can be just words. At that
time, I never imagined that in these moments I was
nurturing my divine gift.

When I look back, though, it is easy to see the pat-
tern. I sparkled when I was communicating my passions. Even though my passions have changed since
the seventh grade, my God-given spark to communicate has grown. When I chose to be a rabbi, it fit.
Rabbis talk. Usually more than they are supposed to.
It was perfect for me.

Now remember all the moments you felt shleimut. What do they have in common?

At first glance, it may appear like nothing. Your first lemonade stand and your sister's wedding may seem completely unrelated. But they are linked. Both of those events ignited your soul. They kindled your divine spark.

People think that all clergy are "called" by God. They think that God speaks to clergy just like people speak to us. So I am often asked, "When were you called?" Meaning, "When did God speak to you?" But God never said to me, "Sherre, I call you to serve the Jewish people as a rabbi." God never talked to me like that. But God did talk to me. God told me, many different times and in many different ways, to use my divine spark. That was my calling.

Each one of us has a calling, a divine purpose. We think the term is reserved for clergy because clergy answer to a "higher call." But each one of us has a direct line. Our calling may sound more mundane, but it is just as meaningful.

As a child I went to my rabbi only in a crisis for words of comfort. More often I found comfort at the home of my mother's best friend, Shirley Colodny. I was not the only one. There was a whole group of us who would knock on her door at 3:30 P.M. for some fresh-baked chocolate chip cookies. On any given day, there was lemon cake, rugelach, or kugel. Everything she made was delicious. Most people dismissed her talent. She was just a stay-at-home mom who baked. Except to us, she was our confidante, our friend, our "cookie lady." She always knew how to comfort us. It was her calling, and she expressed it through baked goods. She was just as important to me as my rabbi.

Take the time to review the moments that ignited your spark. I was communicating, Shirley was comforting, what were you doing? What was the theme throughout all your moments?

Maybe it was music. When you learned to play the cello, played in the high school band, wrote a review in *Rolling Stone,* went to a U2 concert. Maybe it was helping the elderly: when you visited your grandparents, volunteered at the nursing home, helped a man cross the street. Maybe it was making people laugh: you were the class clown, the funny waiter who got the biggest tips, the family speechwriter. Each of these moments, however mundane, was teaching you something profound about yourself. They were all revealing your divine spark.

After years of training and even more in the pulpit, I began to think that my calling was to be a rabbi. I was expecting to be in the pulpit forever. Isn't that what real rabbis do?

Except after a while, speaking from the pulpit no longer felt divine. It was a dear friend who brought me clarity. He reminded me that my spark was my ability to communicate with people. An ability that was not limited to the pulpit. I could do what I loved in many different ways. The pulpit was one option. Once I opened up my mind, the possibilities were limitless.

If you are having trouble finding the thread, you may be focusing on the wrong things. You may need to ask someone else. They may see something in you that you have overlooked or have never valued. They may see in you what you cannot see in yourself. Honor what they say. Don't belittle their assessment. I know Shirley dismissed her talents. She did not think of her gift as divine. But years later, we still feel her glow.

You may think you are an exception: God gave everyone else in the world a divine spark, but you are spark-free. But the truth is, God did not forget you. We are all diamonds.

When in doubt, look to the people whose sparks you can easily see. You know the ones. Their sparks can help us see our own. They can remind us when we may have forgotten.

Look to the people you most admire, your Aunt Gladys, your fifth-grade teacher, or Golda Meir. They are bringing their divine sparks to the world. Now it is your turn. Use them as models. Once you know what awakens your soul, you are ready to light up the world. Ready to make a new plan. One that can't fail. One in which you and God are partners and laugh together.

What is your calling?
What has God been trying to tell you?

VII

ENGAGING UP

STEP EIGHT

Step eight is an adventure. It is when you actually
leap, both in faith and in action. This step teaches
you that the paradigm is not succeed or fail, win
or lose, black or white. Rather, in this step, you
learn a new way to think. Taking a chance, moving
in a specific direction, being in action is in itself a
success, regardless of the final result. All movements,
from baby steps to flying leaps, can make a dramatic
impact. Each one moves us forward and helps us
along our divine path.

❧

Part of the American dream is to own your own
home—the land of the free is not free enough until

you have your own domain, which is yours and yours alone. And yet, owning a home can sometimes feel like the very antithesis of freedom. When the roof leaks, the paint peels, and the trees need trimming, you are responsible. You are the one who has to make the arrangements. You need to find the time to do it yourself, or to hire workers, oversee the job, and pay the costs. When you rent and the paint chips, it is not your problem. It is your landlord's. You don't like the way it was fixed? You move. Even though we know all of this, we still want to own. With ownership comes pride, autonomy, and fulfillment.

The same is true of your life. Owning your life plan is even better than owning a home. You do not need money for a down payment, time to research the best property, or the go-ahead from your family. All you need is you.

If you wait for someone else to fix your life plan, you will wait a lifetime. Sure, it would be nice to have someone jump in and tell you what to do, how to do it, and how it will turn out. And there is always that one person who thinks he or she knows the best way, i.e., your mother's "friend." But eventually you resent that person. She does not truly know what will spark your soul. Often what people advise us is what sparks *their* souls. Only you can rescue yourself. Only you can make the life you imagined. Even God cannot do it without you.

It is time to become the owner of your plan. It is time to realize that your life plan begins with you. You have to do the footwork. This can seem overwhelming. With this power comes responsibility. It can feel tiring, sometimes impossible. Where do I begin? What if I make a mistake? What if I disappoint myself? Who will I blame? You have only you to work it out.

But owning your life plan will give you a far greater sense of purpose and meaning than you can imagine. Rather than waiting for the perfect time, the perfect situation, the perfect opportunity, you will make it happen. And with you in charge, far more will become possible.

Now is the time to take action. Become the owner of your life plan. From this moment, make sure the plan is no longer happening to you. *You* are making it happen. *You* set the tone. *You* make the agenda. *You* are the boss.

"Fine" Is Not Enough

For most of my adult life, I worked for someone else.

As an unpaid summer intern I emptied trash cans on Capitol Hill. In my first "real job," my main responsibility, it seemed, was to learn to make coffee like a Starbucks pro, even though I drink only tea. As I got older and paid my dues, my responsibilities and jobs grew. Eventually I got the good office, the assistant, the freedom to come and go as I please. I had it all: respect, good pay, and health insurance. It seemed that I'd finally arrived—that I was the CEO of my plan.

But somewhere along the way, I changed, and my plan stayed stagnant. The meaning I once felt was slightly dulled. It no longer felt like God and I were in sync. Since I had all the trappings of "success," since I had gotten all the things I thought I wanted out of my working life, I kept telling myself that it was okay. I told myself I was working for God. But though I may have been working *for* God, I was no longer working *with* God. I no longer felt like I was running my life plan; it was running me. When people asked me how I was doing, I said, "Fine." But I knew what "fine" really meant, and I knew that "fine" was not enough.

I started to explore what might reignite my soul. The early changes were minor. I stopped taking as many late meetings. I set aside time each week to study. I made a social lunch once a month. I thought no one would notice. Who was paying that much attention to my comings and goings?

Except from the beginning, other people noticed my restlessness. People told me to settle down, to appreciate all that I had accomplished. They told me I was so lucky. They asked, "What more could you want?" Sometimes it was easier for them to imagine that, rather than wanting more, I wanted less, that I could not handle everything, that the stress was too much for me.

"Settle down." Just hearing those words depressed me. No wonder Peter Pan never wanted to grow up. Why "grow up" only to "settle down"? It felt like if I settled down, I would get stuck. What I realized is that the mark of maturity is to engage up, not to settle down. It is to believe that your divine spark has the potential to grow endlessly. It has the power to transform you and the world.

I started to reflect on how much had happened since I began my job. I began my job as a single twenty-something. Over the years, I married, my father died, I got pregnant, I had a son, I got pregnant again, I had a daughter, my mother got cancer, I got pregnant again. And these were just some of the most obvious changes. I was not the same person as when I'd started, almost ten years earlier. My job had remained the same. But I had not. It no longer fit.

I needed a new strategy. In the business model, managers focus on strategic plans that incorporate not only their desired objectives but also the influences of the world around them. So too I needed to make a strategic plan that incorporated the internal and external fluctuations of my life and to change accordingly.

The nature of being a rabbi is pretty static. It is hard to reinvent yourself in a pulpit. I tried. I thought enough small changes, like reorganizing my office or adjusting my schedule, would suffice. I would find the good balance. But the more I made minor changes, the clearer it became that I needed a bigger one.

Transformation can be empowering. In the Jewish tradition, the rabbis say that one good deed leads to another. So too one change leads to another. I started to make bigger changes. I went to Israel twice a year to study. I began to publish more articles. I started lecturing on spirituality at venues outside my congregation, reaching out to people from more varied backgrounds and points of view.

God was talking, and I was listening.

> *Be strong and resolute; do not be terrified or dismayed, for God is with you wherever you go.* —Joshua 1:9

CHOOSE LIFE

One day a friend of mine who works in television called, asking if I would consider trying out for a two-minute segment on a new cable show. Up until this point, all I knew about television was how to turn it on and that I loved to watch it. The opportunity sounded fun, but I was apprehensive. I had hated acting in school. I never wanted to pretend to be someone else. Living in L.A., I had heard horror stories about the soul-sucking Hollywood machine. On top of this, I was pregnant with my second child and felt as big as a house. Even my maternity clothes were too tight.

I had a choice. I could interview. Try something

new. Challenge my perceptions. Take a risk. Get rejected or get hired. Or I could stay home. Tell my friend I am too pregnant. I have no experience. It is just not a good time.

We all have a choice each day of our lives. The choice is whether to live or to die. Living means to be open, to take chances, to chase our passion and light our soul. Dying means staying stuck, closed, hiding in the recesses of our comfort zone. In the Torah, God makes it clear: "I set before you life and death, choose life." God wants us to choose the path that is risky, daunting, unknown, exhilarating. With this teaching in mind, I told my friend I would be there.

When I arrived, I was a fish out of water. I was surrounded by shiny personalities with obvious experience at auditioning. They knew the cues, the slang, the process. I knew nothing. I thought about walking out. No one would have noticed. But my curiosity outweighed my fears. I waited my turn. When it came time for me to go in, I realized that while the cameras were new for me, the task was not. I just needed to be myself and communicate my passion. Here was an opportunity to bring my divine spark to the people watching.

When I got a call a few months later that the producers wanted me to fly to Atlanta and New York to tape segments, I was delighted and terrified. While it sounded fun to play hooky from my life, I had no clue what I was doing. What would my congregants think? Would my kids be upset that I was gone? Would I sound smart enough?

But being there felt right. And when I got home, I was reinvigorated. Who knew that I could succeed in something so far out of my comfort zone? When they called to tell me that the show would never air, I was not deflated as I would have expected. I was still proud that I'd tried something entirely new. I had been open. I'd done something that I never thought possible.

When I reported the news, my husband and I ended up laughing together.

I Love New York

The culture, the subways, the pace, the energy—I love everything about New York City. So I was delighted when the show was given a second chance. On my first visit, I was walking through Central Park savoring each moment. It was spring. The weather was beautiful, the flowers were blooming. The park was buzzing. It was obvious I was from out of town as I greeted every stranger with an exuberant smile and hello. Mostly, I was met with dismissive glances. I noticed then that, while I was looking up, a lot of other people were looking down.

Three trips later, I stopped noticing the details in the park. Instead of being the excited tourist, I became a worker bee, and I soon blended in with everyone else. I began to treat New York as a job, not an adventure. As soon as I knew the drill, I followed it with precision. I did not deviate. I ate the same thing at the same coffee shop every morning. I left the same tip. I walked the same route. I said the same thing to the doorman. I was no longer seeing the wonderful mix of faces of people from all over the world bustling about. I did not notice when I walked by Carnegie Hall and Lincoln Center. I literally stopped looking up.

The danger of routine is that we do not see the world around us. Our focus becomes linear and narrow. We know what we are doing, where we are going, and each day is spent following that schedule. In no time, we stop thinking. Our habits become so ingrained that we do not even remember the actions we take. Putting the token in the bus, locking the door behind us, even drinking morning coffee. We know that we did it, we just don't remember.

Each new year in Judaism we blow into the shofar, a ram's horn. The sound is (as you might expect) unlike any other. It comes from a ram! The blast is supposed to jar us from our routine, because it is easy to get caught in the sameness of our days. I often say, "Same action, same result. Different action, different result." It is that simple. Try something new. Brush your teeth with your other hand, cross your legs the opposite way, walk home from work. At first it may feel awkward and uncomfortable. We find comfort in our routines.

Change feels strange. Just think about the time you cut your hair really short. It wasn't just a haircut, it was a statement to the world, "I am changing." Immediately, you were a different person. When we alter our routine, we are awakened. We are forced to look up. We open ourselves to new possibilities, new opportunities, new ways to see the world. We are no longer seasoned veterans, we are excited newcomers.

Start by actually looking up when you are walking. Greet people with a smile, even if you live in New

York. You never know whom you might see. What person may cross your path. What sight might inspire you.

My husband has a knack for looking up. He is good at leaving his comfort zone. He has traveled to Tibet, and he has worked in Bosnia and Japan. A boy from Baton Rouge, Louisiana, he puts most city folk to shame. But when he was dating, he followed the same path over and over, and he remained single. I would never fit into his mold. Had we met under different circumstances, he would not have seen me. As it turned out, our paths had crossed once before and neither one of us took notice. But in a moment when he was so far from his routine, in a new state with different friends and new circumstances, he was forced to look up. And when he did, we found each other.

JACOB'S LADDER

When Jacob left his parents' home, he was not journeying to settle down.

He was starting an adventure. His first night alone, he had a dream. He dreamed about a ladder that reached from the earth all the way up to God, with angels climbing up and down it. Jacob's ladder represented all the opportunities that he had in front of him to reach new heights. He already had taken the first step by leaving home. This dream reminded him that even if the ladders were not always obvious, they were always there. There was always another rung to climb.

You may not dream of angelic ladders, but they are all around you, ready for you to ascend. Some ladders may seem impossible to climb. Some may feel dangerous. Some may appear too short. Some may seem totally unrelated to your life. But every ladder counts. With each rung, it will become easier and your perspective will change. Your world will start to look more and more different.

Akiba's ladder looked really high. He was a forty-year-old bachelor who had a decent job herding sheep. He had settled down, until he saw Her. She was the woman of his dreams. She was the one. He was immediately head over heels and planned their future. "I will marry her, and together we will live as husband and wife, shepherd and shepherdess." Except the woman he wanted to marry was the daughter of a great scholar who opposed the marriage. Her father wanted nothing to do with a poor sheep herder; he wanted his daughter to marry someone of higher stature, someone who had at least studied.

Akiba had a choice. He could stay put in his life, or he could engage up with a new plan, one that would get the girl. Keeping status quo would have been an easier path. He could have continued his life as he knew it. Nothing gained, nothing lost. Instead he decided to climb one rung of the ladder to see where it would lead.

With no previous education, Akiba began to study. For seven years he studied and studied and studied. He returned to the girl's father confident that he had met the requirements. No such luck. Her father was unimpressed. Akiba needed to study more to win her hand. No one ever accused Akiba of being a slacker; he went back to study for another seven years. By the time Akiba turned fifty, he was still single, but he was achieving academic heights he had never imagined. He was engaging up.

In the first century C.E., fifty was not the new thirty; Akiba was old. But when Akiba was fifty-four, her father finally found Akiba suitable for his daughter. Akiba's plan had never been to become a great scholar. He had never even considered academia. But by taking the risk, by choosing life, he found more than a wife. He ignited his divine spark. He was an okay shepherd but a tremendous scholar. Akiba eventually became one of the greatest scholars of all time. And he got the girl.

Akiba could have said, "I do not need such demanding in-laws." He could have walked away. He didn't. Akiba was open. He was open to suggestions, ideas, and new directions. He was open to change. Open to something that seemed completely ridiculous. He had no idea where it would lead. His father-in-law did not think he could do it. I am sure his family and friends were skeptical. And though he probably felt entirely ill equipped and inadequate, he never let that hold him back.

Without any guarantees, he took the first step up the ladder, and it made all the difference.

TAKING A CHANCE

My grandmother, who worked every day of her ninety-seven years, always told me, "Never leave a job until you have a new one." Feeling a little reckless, I did not follow her advice.

I came to realize that my spark, my desire to communicate spirituality to a wider audience, had become a flame. And while I still felt the spark in the pulpit, that was not where it was growing. I started to wonder if juggling the pulpit with my other interests made sense.

Was I willing to leave the known for the unknown? How would I make a living? What would people think? It was not a black-or-white choice. No major decisions are. The pulpit was good—yet taking a chance felt better.

I had been debating what path I should follow in my life for over a year when enlightenment came via an unusual source—my favorite pair of jeans. Except for some bizarre exceptions, most women a few months after giving birth would not feel ready to model down their hallway, let alone on a runway. My daughter was almost a year old before I was back to my goal weight, and the whole time I couldn't wait to put on my favorite jeans. When it seemed the moment had finally arrived for their next public appearance, they just did not fit. I could not understand why. I had worn the jeans for years. I loved them. They were the good-butt jeans, the skinny jeans. But now something was not quite right. As cute as they had once been, after three kids in four years, they just did not work any longer. I had to face it——I needed new jeans.

Recent polls show that people rarely regret the chances that they have taken, even when they did not turn out as planned. The real lingering regret comes from the chances that they did not take.

In Yiddish to be a "Nachshon" means to be an initiator. To take a risk not knowing what will happen. As the Israelites were fleeing the Egyptians, when they reached the Red Sea, they knew they had a problem. They did not know how to swim. If they jumped in, they were going to drown. If they stayed on dry land, they were going to be killed. With everyone standing frozen around him, it was Nachshon who jumped into the sea. He had never swum, but he knew it was a chance that he had to take. When he was up to his neck in the sea, the waters parted and the Israelites escaped.

Each one of us has moments when we need to be a Nachshon and take a chance. Maybe it is as significant as quitting your job or as seemingly minor as letting your kids ride the bus. Both instances require us to take an action without knowing the results.

Abraham Joshua Heschel said, "Judaism does not ask its followers to take a leap of faith, it asks them to take a leap of action." If you wait to feel inspired, there will be no end to the waiting. You think, "I will have the difficult conversation when the time is right." A year later, you still have not found the right time. Most of the time, action has to come before faith. You have to "act as if" before you actually are.

Be courageous; leap into action.

So do you leap into a new job as soon as your boss hassles you? Do you leave your marriage for the alluring assistant as soon as your husband irritates you? Sometimes it is difficult to distinguish which chances are worth taking.

There is a difference between a momentary excitement and what really ignites your soul. There can be opportunities that you don't take because they are not in line with your divine spark.

When Leon married, he married well. His bride's family ran a successful company. Right away, he was invited into the business. His father-in-law made it clear. Within ten years he could retire. Passion, shmassion. It was the opportunity of a lifetime. Saying yes meant that he would be respected and rich. Saying no meant a life of financial uncertainty and the wrath of his in-laws. But Leon knew in his heart that the work did not light his spark. In the end, he declined.

Though he had occasional moments of remorse, he knew he had made the right decision.

For Leon to say no took tremendous courage. Sometimes you will take the right risks and occasionally the wrong ones. As you honor the partnership between you and God, you will realize that honoring your spark is what is authentic. Learning which risks fit and which ones don't will only make your spark brighter.

> *Break your routine.*
> *Look up and see all the ladders around you.*
> *Take a step up.*

INTEGRATING

When I first learned to ski, I imagined that an adorable instructor would take me down the hill in my sexy skiing outfit and sleek sunglasses, and I would feel the wind rushing through my hair. But that is hardly what happened. There was no hill. No swoosh. No thrill.

We Plan, God Laughs

The first thing the instructor taught me was how to fall on a level slope. He knew the most important thing in skiing is getting up after you fall. So we fell and got up. Fell and got up until I was completely covered in snow and bruises. Then we called it a day.

When I actually felt the first buzz of swooshing down the hill on skis, I forgot all the falls that had come before. I just felt the thrill. But if I had never learned to get up after falling, I would never have skied.

In Hebrew, the falls and barriers in our lives all have one name, "klippot." Klippot, literally "shells," not only stop us but also protect a meaningful center. They force us to push through our comfort zone in order to help us find what's deep within us. Sometimes the obstacles feel insurmountable, but the Jewish tradition teaches that behind every klippah is an angel of God helping us to move through the barriers. There is a famous teaching from the Midrash that every blade of grass has an angel striking it and telling it, "Grow, grow."

So too when you take a chance, there is an angel of God right there helping you to get back up after you fall. The angel of God is helping you move forward so you can feel the thrill. It is part of the experience. In all strategic plans, the challenges along the way deepen the process. They are information. They let you know what works to engage up and what does not.

At this point, you may feel like you have fallen enough times. You may be saying, "All right already, I am ready to ski." The Talmud teaches that "You cannot fully understand Torah unless you have stumbled in it." The more you stumble, the better you ski. Because the more you know how to handle the falls, the more you can integrate them into your runs. They enable you to ski any mountain.

Cheryl got engaged after three months. Everyone was shocked. "How do you know he is the right one?" "Isn't it a bit fast?" "You barely know him. Shouldn't you date longer?" When I spoke to her, I asked the same questions. She told me that she had sixteen years of practice. Sixteen years of gathering information, learning from all the past relationships, both good and bad. All those years, she had taken the knowledge from previous men to the next one until she met her soul mate. She knew when it fit because she had integrated her history into her present.

> *Integrate your past. Mistakes are moguls. They are small hills that force you to navigate the future terrain differently. Once you have mastered one, you know better how to handle the next. In skiing and in life, you can't avoid the bumps. They are inevitable. They are practice. But if you integrate them, they will make what comes next easier to navigate. They will enable you to find the right fit.*

Tweaking

I am always amazed how a subtle adjustment in my prescription eyeglasses can change my entire outlook (and get rid of a headache). Start small. Make a few tweaks here and there before you quit your job to climb Mount Everest.

Ron came from a family of lawyers—his brother, both his parents, his grandfather, even his great-grandfather. He had always loved basketball. He played in high school, college, even law school. But as work got busier and busier, basketball faded away. Besides, he had learned a lot about precedent, and he knew it was not likely that he would become the first

Jew in the NBA. Even still, he fantasized about what his life would be like if he was able to make basketball his career.

One day, a colleague mentioned that his daughter's basketball coach was sick and they were looking for a substitute coach for the day. Ron jumped at the chance. He loved it. He decided to look for more opportunities to sub at the local school. A few years later, he is coaching a local team. Three mornings a week before his "real job" begins, he starts his day by sparkling on the court, and that spark is lighting up all aspects of his life. Basketball never became his full-time job, but it keeps his flame bright.

Judaism has 613 mitzvoth, rules. Some are impossible to follow. Others take a lifetime to learn to practice. They cover everything from how you eat to how you divorce to how you die. So when people come to me and ask, "How can I be more Jewish?" there are a lot of things I could say. If I mapped out just the rules for eating (keeping kosher) and had them try to follow those rules immediately, the inquirers would never come back. Instead, I suggest a few realistic possibilities that they can implement now, with the hope that those small tweaks will inspire them to ask for more.

What makes tweaking an effective method is that the initial change can be easily incorporated. It does not tip your entire life over. In fact, it may be so subtle that it feels insignificant. That's okay, because it lets you know that next time you can take an even bigger step. What is most important is that you take a step in a direction, any direction.

Throughout the holiday of Sukkot, Jews shake a *lulav,* a palm branch held together with willow and myrtle twigs and an etrog, a funny-looking citrus fruit. Jews shake the lulav in six directions: up, right, back, left, front, and down to symbolize that God dwells in every direction. So too when you take a step in a direction to engage your divine spark, God is with you.

The Jewish tradition teaches that if we open the door of repentance only the width of the eye of a needle, then God will open it wide enough for carriages and wagons to pass through. With a tiny tweak, you can make a dramatic opening.

My yoga teacher, Zoe, started her career as a reporter. After graduating from college, she took an internship in Turkey. She stayed on, and within a few years, she became one of the lead anchors. It was there that she did a story that took her to India. While investigating the story, she met a yogi. She returned to Turkey and began taking yoga classes. She loved them. Each day she looked forward to that hour more than any other. Eventually she moved back to the United States without a job. A passing acquaintance mentioned to her that a local yoga studio was training teachers. She enrolled. Not long after, teaching yoga became her full-time job.

It is time to make small tweaks and see where they lead. What can you tweak today?

COURAGE

When my mother told me that she was thinking about leaving my father, I sent her a card. The front read, "To a courageous woman." My mother threw it in a drawer and never mentioned having received it. When I eventually asked her about it, she said, "I am not courageous." She thought she would not be courageous until she left.

But she already was. Her willingness to admit that she needed to make a change in her life was truly an act of courage. It was the first step. That moment made me see my mother in a new light. She was no longer just my mother; she was a brave woman engaging up.

For her, the moment did not feel so dramatic. She was just thinking about leaving my father; she was far from walking out the door. But that moment changed her life forever. At that moment, she started on a new path, one on which she was in control.

> *In case you never receive a card that says "To a courageous person . . . ," consider this my card to you: You are brave. Believe it. You know something needs to change and you are willing to address it. This is the badge of courage. This is the beginning of living the life you want.*

IX

FINDING MEANING

STEP NINE

In step nine you uncover a powerful truth. You
belong here. You are an agent of the divine here on
earth. With this understanding you are empowered.
You embrace your true purpose. You discover that
by living your divine path, you shape the world,
and improve it. In turn, it continues to shape and
improve you. As Shakespeare said, "Joy's soul lies in
the doing."

In this step you discover that living your divine path
goes far beyond just you. Step nine is priceless, for
it teaches that you are here for a reason. You matter.

❧

This year I look different. Sure I do. I just had my third baby, and I have not slept in months. So when people start their conversations with "You look different," I assume the worst. At first I was surprised that, instead of the empathetic head tilt and a reminder to "take care of yourself too," they said, "You look relaxed, content, younger, better." They assumed it was because I no longer sat in an office for sixty hours a week. They thought now, with all the time in the world, I was spending hours beautifying. But they were mistaken. I used to go to one office and do one job. Now I have many jobs and many offices to balance. My time is more limited than ever. But I agree. I look different.

My soul is on fire. I am pursuing my divine purpose. I feel shleimut. That is what people are noticing. There is no English word that accurately describes the look of shleimut. People give it all kinds of names: "happiness," "peace," "inner beauty," even "thin." This is the first sign that your plan is right. You exude shleimut from the inside out.

What people find confusing is that I have "the look" but I have no results that they can see. There is no finished product. Most people think they will get the look only once they have reached their goal. They never imagine that the process itself can give it to you. The look comes when you are pursuing your divine purpose. The results become less important.

Recently my son was telling a classmate that his father was a doctor and his mother, a writer. I was surprised. I am a rabbi, not a writer! But every day, he sees me writing a book, so in his eyes, I am a writer. When I heard his comment, it was jarring. I laughed at the thought of calling myself "an author." Who am I to call myself an author?

It reminded me of my first day in the pulpit. Every time I heard "Rabbi," I thought the speaker was referring to someone else. Most of the day I felt like giggling. Rabbi? Me? No. But the next day, it felt a tiny bit more fitting. In time, I found myself responding to my title and signing my name—Rabbi Sherre Zwelling (later Hirsch)—without even thinking because being a pulpit rabbi then indicated I was pursuing my divine purpose.

My stepfather is a sailor. He started sailing when he was five, and at seventy he is showing no sign of quitting any time soon. He has taught us that flowing is not always linear. You do not take the boat out, sail, and return. Each day is different. There are waves and waters to navigate. You have to consider the weather, the conditions, the other boats, even yourself on any given day. What makes him a great sailor is that, for sixty-five years, he has never expected the water to remain the same. The seas have changed around him and within him. His passion and love for sailing have increased as he has learned how to maneuver the boat. When he was five, he did not know what he knows now, that he would sail into his seventies flowing with the waves and finding the water more meaningful with each passing year.

We know our divine plan is working when it flows. One of the roots of the word "prophet" (navi) in Hebrew is "nava," to flow forth. When we are becoming the prophets that God knows we can be, our divine sparks flow forth in the world.

Rabbi Yose ben Kisma was the man. He was a rabbi's rabbi. He was the one other rabbis went to with questions, dilemmas, and concerns. He was the rabbi others aspired to become. He had the entire package. His community loved him, and he loved them in return.

One day when he was traveling on vacation, he met a rich man from a nearby community. The rich man saw Rabbi Yose's talent, acumen, and passion. He saw a man who could transform his community from a small star to a grand light. He knew that Rabbi Yose just had to be their rabbi. He imagined if he offered two times, four times, or even ten times Rabbi Yose's current salary, at a certain point Rabbi Yose could not refuse.

The man offered Rabbi Yose the greatest salary of all time. Rabbis were not well-paid. The offer was irresistible. Rabbi Yose's community began to mourn. They knew it would be impossible for him to refuse. They began to search for a new rabbi.

But then the unexpected happened. Rabbi Yose refused the job. He knew that his spark was ablaze and that a move would be a mistake. He knew where he belonged—with his community. He decided to stay and to continue lighting his own life and the lives of the people he loved.

Rabbi Yose knew something that we often forget. When we are pursuing our divine plan, it fits. It is authentic. It resonates in our soul. Your spark nourishes you. It sustains you. It gives you balance.

In Judaism, there is a tradition that we all should carry a slip of paper in each pocket. In the right pocket the note reads "I am the center of the world." And in the left pocket the note reads "I am but dust and ashes." Each day, each moment we are supposed to

walk through life with the awareness of the messages
on these slips of paper, the greatness and the small-
ness of our presence on this earth. We are supposed
to feel the balance between being the most important
person in the world, one of God's greatest creations,
and the most insignificant person in the world, one
of billions.

When you have turned your divine spark into a
flame, you carry that balance into everything you do.
You carry your spark into situations to make them
better. You carry it with you to enhance already great
places.

> *The Baal Shem Tov said, "In whatever you do, let a spark of
> the holy fire burn within you so that you may fan it into
> a flame."*

VALUING THE PROCESS

We all question ourselves sometimes. Don't we?

"What am I doing with my life?" "Am I in the job
that's best for me?" "Is this a good relationship for me?"

"Am I a good parent?" "Will (blank) make me happy?" We never get any guarantees. Some days we each feel doubtful. We feel the pressure. Our loved ones feel what we are feeling, as do those with whom we have only passing contact. It is not always easy to brush it off.

Most people want to know, "Have you reached the top yet? Did you get the gold star? Did you win? Did you come in first?" When you do, then people acknowledge your achievement.

I went to high school with a girl training to be the next Chris Evert. She played tennis before and after school, on weekends, even when it rained. She never had a day off. She couldn't swim; it would soften her muscles. She couldn't sleep over; the next morning she would be too tired to practice. She lived and breathed tennis, and at sixteen, she turned pro. Suddenly everyone wanted to be her best friend. She became the most popular girl overnight. Her new friends were not aware of her regimen and rules. They had not been involved in the years beforehand. But they wanted a piece of her.

By the time we graduated, she was burning out, but since she had already turned pro, she could not even get a college tennis scholarship. Now, being her best friend was not as interesting. She was no longer going to win Wimbledon. When she wanted to make a comeback, people wanted to know only one thing, was she winning again?

The Bible knows better. The five books of Moses end at the beginning. You would think at the end, Moses and the people would be living in the land of Israel. After many generations, years of travels, and lots of hardship, all right already, get to the land. Instead, Moses dies and the people are still waiting to enter the land. It is so not the Hollywood ending. The Bible is letting us know that the process is as important as the final destination.

Recently I climbed a rock wall with five other women, ages thirty-five to seventy. (No, we were not making an escape.) None of us had ever climbed before. It was billed as a "trust-building" experience, designed to unite us as a group. It sounded great, until we saw the wall. It was much higher than the guide had described. There was no gradual slope—it went straight up. It was not the ladder of our dreams, although it did appear to reach the heavens. They strapped us in to harnesses and assured us that there was no chance of getting hurt. Still, none of us felt the least bit cheery.

Finding Meaning

Why were we afraid? Maybe we felt there was more at stake than just falling. Each of us feared that she would be the only one not to reach the top, that she would be ashamed and embarrassed.

When we finally got started, it was even harder than we had expected, but we all climbed farther than we imagined we could. Only one woman made it to the top, and when she did it was as thrilling as if we had made it ourselves.

That night the women who did not climb with us asked, "How did you do?" Everyone answered sincerely, "Phenomenally!" Of course, to the people who asked, that answer meant that everyone had reached the top. But the six of us knew that success isn't just about reaching the top or getting the gold star.

When your divine plan is working, you are focused on the ascent. You are focused on the climb, the way up, the action. You are not focused only on the top, a future goal that may or may not materialize. Although you may not be close to the top, or even be sure where the top is, when people ask "How are you doing?" you will answer "Phenomenally!"

We Plan, God Laughs

Discovering Abundance

There is always a "but." He is the greatest guy, *but* he can't commit. She is supersuccessful, *but* she is catty. He is a babe *but* not the sharpest tool in the shed. Why do we feel the need to belittle the success of others? Does doing so really make us look and feel better?

We act like there is a limited supply of beauty, love, friendship, success, and meaning in the world. If she is beautiful, then why does she deserve to be successful too?

Jill was thriving as a psychologist. Her colleagues praised her; her patients loved her. She was proud of her work. When it came time for a raise, she had no doubt that she would be compensated fairly. So she was shocked when she learned that she would receive only a nominal increase. The company was thriving. What had she done wrong?

What she found out was that it had nothing to do with her. Her superior was paid three times her salary, and he too was due for an increase. She learned after the fact that he demanded that his salary remain three times hers. He had presumed an increase for her would mean less for him. Had she been compensated fairly, their salaries would still have recognized them both appropriately. But he feared not only that her increase would threaten his own but also that she would gain more influence and importance and he would have less.

A mentality of scarcity can present itself in numerous ways. We can become jealous and fearful of others without even knowing them. We can become unreasonably competitive and nasty. In its worst form, a mentality of scarcity can lead us to rejoice in other people's pain.

When we are on our divine path, it no longer feels like there are a limited number of pieces in the pie. Now we can see that the pie is much larger than we thought, and we can always bake more. There are so many flavors of pies: apple, chocolate, raspberry . . .

It no longer feels like what another possesses takes away from what we can get. Rather, when people succeed, we celebrate. When they fall, we empathize. We even help them stand again. It is the opposite of our behavior in the past. We go from a mentality of scarcity to a mentality of abundance.

We know that someone else's finding love does not

decrease our chances of doing so. In fact, their experience may enhance our possibilities. Her boyfriend may have an adorable brother. We know that when our friend's invention takes off and he becomes a billionaire, his success does not diminish our own possibilities, it enhances them. We begin to say, "If he can, so can I," rather than "If he did it, then I did not." We begin to see that others' success may increase our own.

In the Jewish tradition, the reading of the Torah is divided into weekly portions so over the course of a year, we have finished all five books. When we have completed each book, it is customary to rise and to repeat out loud the words "Hazak, Hazak, v'nitchazek," "Be strong, be strong, and let us be strengthened." The message is that the Torah strengthens us as we strengthen it. It is a mutual relationship. So too when we are on our divine path, we see the people around us as sources of strength. We are strengthened by them, and they are strengthened by us.

We willingly share. We stop hoarding. We lift others. When their light shines, we value it, we respect it, we embrace it. It enables us to shine even more.

FINDING MEANING

God never asked Adam and Eve in the Garden of Eden, "Are you happy?"

Today we think happiness is our right. After all, it says so in the Declaration of Independence. We have "certain unalienable Rights, that among these are Life, Liberty, and the Pursuit of Happiness." But the pursuit of happiness alone is a luxury. Happiness is ephemeral. You can be happy in one moment and not in the next. For what makes you happy today may not tomorrow. Roses after a great date make you happy, the same flowers after a disastrous one just annoy you.

God understands the limits of happiness. All parents understand the limits of happiness. My son, husband, and I recently went to a carnival. My son could not have been happier. He loved the bumper cars, the roller coaster, the popcorn, the cotton candy. The next day, when I told him we were not going back, he was miserable. How could I have given him so much happiness just to take it away? A week later, when I thought the memory was long gone, my son said to me, "Can we go back to the carnival?" I did not want to say no, so instead I asked, "What was your favorite part?" He answered, "Spending time with you and Daddy without Eden and Alia (his sisters)." The carnival made him happy, but the special time with us gave him something more, something deeper.

No one is happy all the time. And the ones who seem to be, you just don't trust. If you have children, then you know it is impossible to be happy every second. Being a parent is the hardest job on the planet. Children talk too much. They misbehave. They are costly. Mine make me want to scream at times. However, generation after generation, we reproduce. We bear children, adopt children, some of us will do anything to have one because a child brings yet another spark to our world. Children can fill our lives with meaning.

Finding meaning is what makes us feel phenomenal. You know even when you are not smiling 365 days of the year that your plan is right when it gives you meaning. Your plan is not something that just makes you happy—it is something that touches your soul, something that gives you a sense of purpose.

God wants you to live a life of meaning. God wants you to bring your divine spark to its full brightness. God is your partner in this quest. Now you and God are in cahoots. You are on the same page. You talk. You hang out. You are in sync. Just as God helped you to discover your divine spark, God helps you to keep it lit. With each passing day as you are fulfilling your divine purpose, instead of feeling farther from God, you feel closer.

It is no longer just about crying out to God for help. It is no longer just about seeking God when you feel alone. Rather you and God feel connected. You seek God just as much as God seeks you. Martin Buber, an Austrian Jewish philosopher whose work focused on interpersonal relationships and community, said, "When we pray we speak to God, when God listens, God speaks to us." The more you sync with God, the easier he is to hear.

God has brought me laughter; everyone who hears will laugh with me. —Genesis 21:6

QUESTIONING

STEP TEN

Every Passover, we focus on questions rather than
answers. The message of the holiday is, "No matter
what, keep asking." Blind faith is just that, blind.
When you have reached this step and have more
questions than ever, know that you are on the right
path. This may feel confusing or frustrating, because
we want answers. We want to know, without a
shadow of a doubt, that this path is right. Paul
Tillich said that doubt is not the opposite of faith,
it is an element of faith. Doubts and questions are
what make your divine path dynamic. They are
what have motivated you to come this far. If you are
afraid to ask and reassess, what feels fresh today may
feel stale tomorrow.

We Plan, God Laughs

If you are the one who always sat in the front row of class, always took notes, and always did the extra-credit work just in case, you might be disappointed with what I am about to say. You can follow all the instructions to devising a divine plan and still find it does not go as planned.

You Are Not Alone

In Judaism, the way to enlightenment is not usually solitary.

In fact, there is only one famous example of a great scholar who found wisdom by isolating himself in a cave. He did not even go there voluntarily. Rabbi Simeon bar Yochai disparaged the Roman government in public and was condemned to death. To escape the decree, he fled with his son to a cave and hid. For twelve years, they studied and they prayed. When they emerged, the first thing that they did was criticize their own people for not being pious enough.

God sent them back to the cave, saying, "You cannot live with other human beings. You are not fit." A year later they reemerged. This time the rabbi was able to be a man among men. He was able to interact with others and eventually become a great Torah scholar.

Basically, it took one of the most brilliant Jewish minds thirteen years to learn that you are not alone in the world. You need to learn to live in relationships with other people.

Some days you may wish you did not have to. Some days you may dream you could isolate yourself and live entirely alone. I did. I spent twelve days on Fantasy Island. Not the one where Tattoo says, "The plane, the plane," but another one. The one where I had to meditate in total silence.

I had dropped out of rabbinical school because it wasn't the spiritual center I had imagined. I was at a loss for how to find that spiritual meaning. A friend suggested I go to a Vipassana meditation center for twelve days and contemplate. Sounded easy and cheap. So I spent twelve days in silent meditation. I did not speak to a soul. I did not look at another—I made not even one gesture. When the teacher instructed us to spend the day focusing on the hairs of our upper lip, I did not laugh. I wanted to, but I didn't. It was forbidden. What I soon learned was that, instead of feeling complete serenity, I felt pain both emotional and physical. Who can sit for so long in one position without human contact? I longed for a nod or a wink from one of my fellow practitioners. I realized that, while I could contemplate and meditate, I could not live my life in isolation. None of us can.

Judaism understands that we don't live in isolation. Part of the greatness and the difficulty of Judaism is that we are never alone. We need a quorum of ten people just to pray. We need three people to formally bless a meal. We need one another. We need community at every stage of life. Even if you feel isolated, you are always part of a bigger world.

LIFE IS MESSY

Being born is messy, and it only gets worse from there. It's how it is. Living in the world can totally mess up our plans. Our plans do not materialize or play out in a vacuum. How we behave, the choices we make, and the dreams we pursue affect others. How they live affects us just as much. We have control only of ourselves. While sometimes we may wish we could control others, the truth is that we can't. In living our divine plan, other people matter.

You might think of yourself as surrounded by concentric circles of relationships. Within the circle that immediately surrounds you are your most closely trusted confidants: perhaps your parents or spouse. In the farthest circle are the strangers, the ones you pass on the street, or even people on the other side of the world whom you may know about only from the news. Of course, the people in the closest circle are directly affected by your choices, dreams, and plans, just as you are affected by theirs. But the people in the other circles affect us as well. With each move we make, our position in the world changes, our relationships change.

As a slightly bizarre example, just look at the process of having to apply for your child to attend preschool. In some cities, such as New York, Los Angeles, and Chicago, you have to apply while your child is still in utero. Even when you act that early, there are no guarantees. A woman I know knew the game. She applied right when her son was born. She enrolled him in toddler classes at the school, she filled out the applications on time, she had letters of recommendation. It was a sure thing. And yet, after all that effort, he was wait-listed. It turned out that, in that year, there were more boy applicants than girls, so it was harder for boys to get in. She had to find another school.

With strangers and preschool, this phenomenon is comical. But when it comes to your job and your family, it is another story.

Philip was a vice president in his company. He felt comfortable and secure until the president's son needed a job. After Philip's years of dedication and hard work, this young gun was sitting in the office next to Philip getting a lot of recognition. Within a year, the son was promoted to senior vice president, above Philip. Suddenly, work became a political minefield.

As a rabbi, I heard about dozens of dramatic instances when people in circles made changes that had dramatic effects not only on themselves but on the other people they loved. Jenny was married for fifteen years. With two kids and a beautiful home, she thought she was living a pretty good life. Until one night, her husband announced between dinner and dessert that he was not in love with her anymore. In just that moment, her plan was almost destroyed. Suddenly there was no room for dessert.

Life can be arbitrary. There are things that happen in the world which are entirely unplanned and incomprehensible.

There are some things that even God does not get. They just happen. We never saw them coming, and we could never have imagined their impact. Sometimes they are tragic, like a bride having a car accident on the way to her wedding. Sometimes they are extraordinary. A child is a musical savant. Sometimes they are completely unrelated to us personally, yet they affect everything in our world. 9/11.

Our plans may not look like we expected because life is happening to us, around us, and within us. This lack of control may feel discouraging. But we may fail to notice that these other factors sometimes work to our benefit. When the president's son was promoted, Philip thought he would be fired and started to look for a new job. But the son saw all his talent, his knowledge, and his importance to the company. Within a few weeks Philip was recognized with more responsibility, a promotion, and a raise. What he thought would be the crushing end was an exciting new beginning.

Lemons do not always become lemonade. It is not the nature of life. But sometimes they do. Sometimes they become lemon pie or the base of some weird jam. Sometimes you look back and say, "Lemons are just lemons," and you drop a slice in your iced tea.

We Plan, God Laughs

Time to Clean

Each year Jews are commanded to clean.

On Passover, the most celebrated Jewish holiday of the year (even more than Hanukkah, who knew?), Jews must clean, clean, and clean. You would think it would be enough to clean the kitchen, but we are commanded to clean our entire homes, our cars, even our workplaces. During the holiday we abstain from eating all bread products to remember the exodus from Egypt. We are not cleaning just for the sake of cleaning, we are emptying our lives of chametz, anything that looks or smells or acts like bread.

The rabbis teach that the process is not just a physical act, it is a spiritual one as well. Each year we must clean out the chametz from our lives. We must shed the behaviors, the negative influences, even the people who are toxic to our souls. As we prepare our homes for the holiday, we prepare ourselves as well. We take stock of our lives by looking at ourselves and our relationships. What is working for us and what is not? Do we need to reshape or relinquish any of our relationships? Do others need a renewed commitment?

Paige came to me for guidance. She told me she was kind of happy but not really. She was twenty-seven and living in an apartment with four college friends. During the day she worked hard. She had become a senior buyer for a major department store and was on her way to becoming a hip young stylist. Her friends had a different plan. Every night they were partying until the wee hours, just like in their college days. Most of them were still living off their parents, so they did not have the same responsibilities Paige did. Paige was excited about the life that she was creating for herself, but she did not want to give up her girlfriends. Except their lives and her life were moving in different directions. She started to live two separate lives, her day life and her night life, but she became increasingly tired, stressed, and resentful. Her college life no longer fit her adult one, and she did not know what to do.

I advised her that sometimes we have to let go in order to move on. This did not mean that she had to fire her friends. Rather she had to redefine the relationship in order to live her life the way she wanted. She thought it was all or nothing. She thought when she moved out, her friends would never speak to her again. But this is not what happened. She did move out, and she moved on. And while their relationships are different, they are still friends.

Sometimes cleaning out the chametz can be daunting. We need to tell our parents to back off. We need to cut off our adult children. We need to set limits with our siblings and our friends. We need to say no.

Either way it is a risk. If we do not say anything, we sacrifice ourselves and our dreams. But if we do say something, we may hurt or alienate someone we love. If you do not do anything, you risk staying stuck or exploding to pieces.

In my mid-twenties, I went to a rabbi for guidance. I had been dating a wonderful man for three years. Everyone, including me, thought we would get married. Except there was a catch. I had to find another career. He did not want to live his life in the public eye as a rabbi's husband. It was understandable. I went to my rabbi, and he advised me that if I loved Jesse, I should leave rabbinical school. I had my own doubts about school anyway, so his advice confirmed my inclination to leave. That is when I dropped out. I decided to travel and eventually live the rest of my life with Jesse.

Everything was going as planned, yet it did not feel

right. The rabbinate still called to me, and I felt suffocated by my decision. I felt as if I had extinguished my spark and compromised my dreams. I knew if I married Jesse, I would be fine. But I wanted more than fine. I wanted to sparkle.

It was one of the hardest decisions of my life. I loved him very deeply, and leaving him was painful. I grieved for a year. But I know that if I'd left myself instead, I would have spent a lifetime grieving.

Sometimes we let go of people we love because we have to love ourselves.
What relationships need to change for you to be on your divine path?

DOUBT

We all doubt. Even Moses doubted. He was supposed to lead the people from slavery into freedom. He doubted himself. He doubted God. A lesser known but equally notable prophet of the Bible, Gideon, also doubted God's plan. He too was supposed to free the people from enemies. He doubted himself and he doubted God.

If both Moses and Gideon, great leaders, were doubtful, then lacking faith must be intrinsic to our nature, part of our genes. You would have expected the heroes of the Bible to have complete faith, blind faith. You would have thought they would have been Zen masters, accepting all of life's challenges with equilibrium, and calm. But they weren't. Both Moses and Gideon needed more.

Every time Moses and Gideon doubted, God would perform a miracle as proof. For Moses, God turned a rod into a snake, and he made water spring from a rock, among others. For Gideon, he made dry wool wet and wet wool dry in an instant—without a hair dryer. (You have to take my word for it, it was a miracle in that time.)

Everyone thinks these acts themselves were miraculous. But what is more amazing is that God kept performing miracles every time he was asked. *That* was a miracle! God could have said, "Enough is enough." God could have said, "I showed you once. I showed you twice. I am done." Instead God kept showing them over and over again to help them believe. God knows that losing faith is human. We all doubt.

God also knows that only with doubt can one gain true faith. When we doubt—God, the process, our divine purpose, ourselves—we are in good company. Our doubts, our questions, our desire for more are what lead us to new insights—to discover the many facets of the spark that God gave us. These insights are God's miracles for you, God's proof that your divine spark can light up the world. They may not be as flashy as the parting of the Red Sea, but they are there.

You already have more faith than you realize. We think faith requires some extraordinary leap and you have your eyes shut when you take it. But we exhibit acts of tremendous faith every day. When we marry it is an act of faith. Whether you dated for five months or five years, you never really know what or who you are getting when you marry. You do not have proof that it will last. You have to have faith. The same is true when you have a child. We can prepare with a birth plan, classes, and baby gear. But it takes faith to grow a baby inside you and then push it out of a small hole. Forget the amount the faith that is required to raise that same child.

Judaism could have been compiled in one book, the Torah. Except in every generation, the people had questions. They had doubts. They wanted clarification, explanations, and more proof. What evolved was a five-thousand-year-old tradition of a living, vibrant dialogue that contains thousands and thousands of pages of conversations and commentaries. It is the years of doubts and questions that have made Judaism expand, grow, and strengthen.

So too your doubts and questions can only strengthen and nourish your plan.

What are some of your doubts?
Can they be a source of strength?

THANKS

Before I got married, Thanksgiving was always the same. My father made the bird. My mother made the stuffing, the gravy, the sweet potatoes, and the cranberry sauce. I knew exactly what was coming, and it always tasted delicious. In my husband's home,

Thanksgiving was always the same. His father made the bird. His mother made the stuffing, the gravy, the sweet potatoes, and the cranberry sauce. When we got married and decided to host Thanksgiving at our home, it should have been a snap.

Turns out in my house growing up, we roasted the bird, my mother's stuffing was fluffy, the sweet potatoes never had marshmallows, and the cranberry sauce came only from a can. At my husband's house, they rotisseried the turkey, the stuffing was made with corn bread, the sweet potatoes always had marshmallows, and the cranberry sauce was homemade.

I figured since I was cooking, I would make my recipes, which I had learned from my mother. Dinner was a disaster. I am no match in the kitchen for either my mother or my mother-in-law. The entire evening my husband was complaining that this was nothing like a real Thanksgiving. My parents mumbled that we should have catered the meal or gone out. There was very little thanks in the atmosphere that day.

Still, I realized then that Thanksgiving was still Thanksgiving. The food was fine. The family was together. We had the blessing of the tradition. Except it was different from what everyone had planned. Everyone had a memory, an idea, a vision of what

Thanksgiving is, and theirs were nothing like mine. Our families could spend all future Thanksgivings unhappy, instead of embracing the new day brought together by the merging of two families.

When my son gets married, I will have to remember as I am sitting at my daughter-in-law's table eating tofu turkey with seaweed stuffing that it is up to me to embrace the difference. (And though it may come back to haunt me, she now has it in writing.)

So too in life, we imagine where our divine plan is headed, and it often goes in a different direction. We may feel disappointed even though there is no real cause. Different feels uncomfortable. When we are uncomfortable, the tendency is to reject. We immediately think this plan could not be right. It feels too strange.

Even though your plan may feel awkward and new, don't reject it. Embrace it.

Ruth was not Jewish, yet she married an adorable, successful Jewish man. Sadly, after ten years, she became a widow. Her mother-in-law, Naomi, assumed Ruth would return to her homeland of Moab in order to marry again. Yet Ruth refused. She clung to Naomi saying, "Wherever you go, I will go, wherever you live, I will live. Your people will be my people and your God my God." Naomi tried to dissuade Ruth, but she still refused.

Even though Ruth did not know what the future entailed, she had found her spark in Judaism. With all kinds of questions—Would she remarry? Would she be able to support herself and Naomi?—she still chose to follow her spark, her love of Judaism, even if it was again going to be new and uncomfortable.

The beginning was not easy. She started to work the fields. But eventually her work led her to meet an old friend of her deceased father-in-law, by the name of Boaz. He was nothing like her deceased husband. But he loved her, and together they had a child. They made a good life together, united in their love for Judaism, their families, and each other.

When Ruth found her divine spark, her Judaism, her plan materialized more differently than she could ever have imagined. Ruth never would have guessed that her husband would die, she would convert to Judaism, marry a much older man, and consider her mother-in-law her own mother.

Every year Jews around the world read the story of Ruth on Shavuot, the holiday that celebrates the giving of the Torah, to recognize her decision to choose Judaism. But maybe we read it for another reason as well. We celebrate Ruth's courage—her decision to follow her spark—to forsake comfort and ease for the unknown possibility of a life of meaning and purpose. We celebrate Ruth in hopes that she will serve as inspiration for us in our own lives, that we will be able to bear the discomfort for what lies beyond.

A Worthy Accomplishment

We may believe our plan is not working because every moment does not feel phenomenal. The spotlight is not shining on us with every move we make. We believed it would feel more spectacular than it does. If this was truly my path, shouldn't I love every single minute?

The truth is that, even when you are on the right path, some of it, sometimes even more than some, is pretty regular. Dina loved working for an international relief organization. At forty her life was filled with meaning. She was raising money to bring goods to people in need. She was traveling the world educating others, meeting interesting people, doing God's work. She sparkled. Except on most days, she was exhausted. She spent more days on a plane than she did on the ground. She was rarely home for Sunday dinner. Some days she could not take one more committee meeting.

Living her divine plan had a lot of regular, and not a lot of dazzle, but it was still right. Work is work. Sometimes you do not want to go. Sometimes it is tiring, uninspiring, and boring. You may not enjoy every second of the process. Here I am writing on days that I do not feel inspired. Sometimes I have to trash the words from the day before. It does not make me happy. In the ideal world, the first draft is the finished product and every word is a masterpiece. After all, I am expressing my divine spark. But in the real world, most words need revising, and inspiration comes in fits and starts. The process is not glamorous.

Even if you have not made your spark your work, your hobbies may be boring. Some days, the things that we most love can seem the most unremarkable. I love doing yoga. It makes me feel peaceful, calm, and centered. It helps light my soul. But some days I make excuses not to go anyway.

> *There is the story of a man complaining to the Baal Shem Tov. The man said, "I am doing what I love. I am studying, praying, following all the commandments to serve God. But still it all feels pretty darn regular." The Baal Shem Tov answered, "You are brilliant. For you understand, it is ordinary and regular and this in itself is a worthy accomplishment."*

BETTER MAY BE DIFFERENT

Rose wanted to make movies. Her mother was an artist. It was in her blood. At eighteen she was serving as a production assistant. By the time she graduated from college, her talents were obvious. Her family was entirely supportive of her dream. When she was accepted to film school, everyone was thrilled. When she made her first film, she was the envy of all her friends. There was no question, she was on her divine path.

Except, something was wrong. Everything was right; yet it did not feel right. Rose decided to make some adjustments, to begin to tweak. She started exploring other areas of the film industry, hoping that it would begin to feel like she expected. It didn't. When she confided in her mother, Rose thought she would encourage her to keep trying, but what her mother advised was that maybe this was not her divine path after all.

Rose grew up in Berkeley in the seventies; she thought she had no lists, no shoulds, no rules. The only thing she was encouraged never to do was sell out, work for corporate America. What she discovered when she really listened was her passion for the law, criminal law in particular. She tried to silence the voice. Had she gone mad? Was she "The Man"?

In law school she shined. She joined every club, wrote for the law journal, and was loved by her classmates, even though she was at least ten years older than most of them, including some teachers. Everyone thought film school was "better" than law school. But for Rose they were just different.

When she was twenty, Rose had dismissed law school. At that time it did not fit, but at thirty-five it made sense. Rose originally thought law school was "bad"; my parents thought rabbinical school was "weird"; most people agree being a doctor is "good." But who is to say what is bad, weird, or good for you?

Our mailman is loved. Vince has worked in our neighborhood for twenty-seven years. He knows the comings and goings of everyone. He knows when there is a new family or when someone dies. I cannot imagine him as anything but our neighborhood mailman. We loved him, but did he love us too? Was he pining to be a fireman? A writer? Or even retired?

One day I asked him. He told me that being a mailman in this community gave him a tremendous sense of meaning. He loved the community, the people, and the job. He loved that he was able to walk outdoors, work alone, and get home early. He could not imagine being anything else. It is easy to judge a mailman. But each day when Vince drops off our mail, what I wish for my son is to feel the same fulfillment on his chosen path.

The rabbis in the Talmud ask, "Will you say that I do great things and my neighbor does small things? For though we do different work, we both rise early and work hard all day. We both recognize that we could not do the other's job. Neither one of us is better than the other so long as we direct our hearts to the divine. We are not better or worse than another, we are just different."

TRY, TRY AGAIN

Who knew it took God many tries before God got creation right?

The Talmud tells us that creating the world was not a piece of cake. First time, God trashed it. Second time he trashed it, third time same thing, and so on and so on. Until by the eleventh time, he was satisfied. He described creation as "good," not awesome, not spectacular, not even great. And even once this world was created, a fair amount of work was still needed. When it was not going as God planned, God flooded the world and started again with just Noah and his zoo.

You might think that your new plan is not divine. You might think that you missed the mark. That God is cheering for everyone but not for you. And once again, you might feel that your new plan is simply wrong. It is not. Just the process of trying to discover your divine spark and make a new plan is right. And I am not merely trying to comfort you. Honest.

Sometimes you have to try again and again before

you get to "good." When God was creating the world, he did not do it the same way over and over and over again. He changed it up. The Midrash teaches that when God finally created the world, he used his divine spark, Torah. At first, he was not sure. He tried to implement his spark one way and it didn't come out like he wished. So he tried again. With each try he discovered how better to use Torah to create the world he envisioned.

Even when we know our divine spark, sometimes it takes many tries to find the best path to follow. Ethan was a great cook. Everyone accepted his invitations for dinner. He could take a seemingly empty cupboard and make delicacies. But he considered screenwriting his love, his passion, his profession. So he decided to combine the two. He wrote a screenplay about a chef, but it never sold. He decided he would take another approach. He tried to open a restaurant, but his writer friends could not afford to invest and it went nowhere. One day when he was out of ideas, Ethan was asked to volunteer in his son's class. The teacher, knowing that he was a great cook, asked if Ethan would teach the students to make a simple recipe. The kids loved his stories just as much as the brownies. Today Ethan runs kids' cooking classes full-time. With many tries, he finally found his path.

But in time, his plan may change again. For now, teaching kids makes sense, but it might not down the line. What Ethan has learned through the process is that it is not about the grand finale. This job may lead to something else. In a few years, he may want to teach adults. He may want to study cooking in France. He may want to revisit that screenplay with his new life experiences. Now it becomes *Kindergarten Cook.*

Judaism teaches in regard to repairing the world that we are not obligated to complete the task. But while we are here, we are not free to desist from it either. Each day we must try to make our world just a little bit better. The same is true in repairing our own lives; we may not reach a given destination, but we must never stop trying.

It may take more time than you anticipate. Everything of true meaning takes time. It takes nine months to have a baby. It takes at least four years to graduate from college. It takes twelve minutes for chocolate chip cookies to bake. If you're five years old, twelve minutes in this case can seem like forever.

Nothing happens overnight. Living the life you

want will take a lifetime. But if you do not keep trying, you may not find it ever gets "good." You may
never find the meaning that will be life sustaining. The
meaning that will let you know that you matter in this
world. That you are divine, and God is overjoyed that
you are here.

May God deliver us from doubt. ——Moses Maimonides

LAUGHING WITH GOD

Here is the bummer. I cannot promise you that the plan you make today will be fulfilled tomorrow. I cannot promise you that your plan will not change again and again. I cannot promise you that your plan will not have many challenging moments and times of doubt.

Here is what I can promise: life will not turn out as you planned. But your divine plan will change your life. And it will change the lives of others. You will discover your true uniqueness through the process. That God made you extraordinary as you are. That you are divine. And that with God you can live a life imbued with meaning and purpose.

Extraordinary You

I have given many eulogies. Many people think that must be the hardest part of my job. Grieving with mourners is painful. When I sit with the family in preparation for the funeral, I often learn more in a few hours about the deceased than I did in years of knowing her or him. Each time I am in awe of the lives that people live. The struggles they overcome. The hurts they bear. The twists and the turns of their paths. The triumphs they celebrated. And the legacies they left. Whether they were community leaders, famous or just famous in their families, all people had divine sparks that illuminated their lives and the lives of others.

My grandmother died at ninety-seven. She had been blessed with a long, long life. My grandmother was not perfect. She could be tough, stubborn, blunt to a fault. She grew up during the Depression, and in many ways she had a very difficult life. She was a widow at thirty and found herself raising three of her children and two stepchildren. Money was tight. Women were not in the workforce. Feminism was not in vogue.

But my grandma Laura had a divine spark. She could turn a nickel into a dollar. She could sell ice to Eskimos. She had inherited a small business from her husband. And with her talent, she made it thrive. Everyone in the small town of London, Ohio, came to shop in her store. As the business grew, she was able to send her children to classes and then to college. When her kids were grown, she continued to work. At ninety, she was the top saleswoman in the sisterhood gift shop at the retirement home.

When she died, we realized how bright Grandma Laura's flame really was. She taught her children, and they in turn taught their children, about the value of work, independence, survival, and financial acumen. Our family can still see and feel her spark.

Grandma Laura mattered. Her spark still illuminates our lives, each year on the anniversary of her death, the yahrzeit, we light a memorial candle to mark the way she lit up our lives. As it flickers for twenty-four hours, we remember her divinity. We remember that she was a creation of God and that she lived a life of meaning.

In Judaism there are no special candles. Whether they were great philanthropists or gave nothing, whether everyone knew them or no one knew them, whether they delivered babies or delivered mail, everyone gets the same ninety-nine-cent candle. As it is lit, it reminds all of us that to God each one of us is equal. We are all extraordinary in God's world.

THE FRUIT OF THE FRUITS

Honi liked to ask questions. In the Talmud, he asked about everything. Whenever he saw something that he did not understand, he asked. One day he was walking on the road and saw an old man planting a carob tree. He asked the man, "How long will it take this tree to bear fruit?" In the desert there was no chocolate; carob was as good as it got. The old man replied, "Seventy years." Honi could not understand. He could not imagine why the man would plant something that would not bear fruit in his lifetime. So he asked the old man, "Why are you doing this?" The old man answered, "When I was born, I found many carob trees that had been planted by my father and grandfather. Just as they planted trees for me, I am planting trees for my children and grandchildren."

The old man was a patient gardener. He knew that

when you plant seeds, you do not always see the fruit right away. He knew he would never taste the carob from these trees, but someone would. Sometimes your divine plan may yield fruit long after you have gone. It may yield results that you could never have expected or even imagined. But you will have left your indelible imprint.

I know. My great-uncle Harry was a respected rabbi in Connecticut. Everyone loved him. And he loved what he did. He used to say that he was born to be a rabbi. He even managed to stay in the same pulpit for fifty years, an almost unbelievable feat. We joked that he was the Cal Ripken of rabbis.

When I was a kid, Uncle Harry used to vacation with us in Southern California during the winters. I remember sitting on his lap, listening to him tell me stories about being a rabbi. Like my parents told me bedtime stories, he told me stories from the Bible, from his days at the seminary, from his time in the pulpit. His stories were riveting. I would wait for him to come each winter to tell me more. Like Honi, I asked all sorts of questions. What happened to the lady who slipped and fell in the grave at the funeral? Is God mad if you go to the movies on the day of rest?

It would never have occurred to either of us that I

was to become a rabbi. In the early seventies, there were no female rabbis. The Reform movement was in conversation. The conservative movement was a few steps behind. In our home, Uncle Harry was not preaching. He was not on the pulpit. But every day Uncle Harry's spark, his profound love of Judaism emanated from deep within him, and it changed us all. His spark inspired my own. And I believe that now he and God are having a good laugh.

My great-uncle's influence continues today with my children, my congregants, and even you. You never know who you will affect when you are living your divine life. For Ruth, following her divine spark, her love of Judaism, led to a new life. But what she never saw was that her son, Obed, became the father of Jesse, who in turn became the father of the great King David. Ruth, a simple woman, would never have believed that her great-grandson would be king.

As proud as Ruth would have been of King David, she would also have reprimanded him for his behavior along the way. He made some mistakes in his effort to be the best king ever. He lost control of his army and himself. He became overwhelmed. He collapsed from exhaustion, his general defied him, he stole his neighbor's wife.

In frustration, David searched within to discover the kind of leader he wanted to be. He realized he had a nation counting on him. He realized he had a son counting on him. He had to rediscover his spark, his passion for justice. In order to fix the world, David needed to fix himself. He needed to put his divine spark into action. He needed to live a life of justice.

Ultimately, this shift changed not only David but the world. King David's legacy is one of justice despite his less than just actions. His son Solomon carried on his father's principles. It was Solomon who built the Holy Temple as a symbol of his father's legacy, justice in the land, and God's presence on earth.

JANET'S STORY

Who knows how many people will be touched by your divine spark?

Janet hardly saw herself as an example for others. She was a career secretary. She was single with two children. She was always on a diet. She went to work. She came home. If you did not need something from her, you barely knew she was there. In her late thirties, Janet decided she was not living the life she wanted.

She thought back to all the moments she felt shleimut. Much to her surprise, they were all connected to accounting. She was the treasurer of her tenth-grade class. She managed her parents' household bills. She did the taxes for her friends and family. She loved overseeing the budgets at work. Even though she had never gone to college, Janet realized she had a knack for numbers. It was her divine spark.

No one had ever encouraged her to go to college. In fact, Janet had been discouraged. Her parents thought college was an impossible dream. When would she find the time? Who would pay for it? How would she manage with her children? Her boss thought that she was not capable. He even told her she was not smart enough. For a while she believed them all.

At thirty-eight, Janet stopped judging herself. She stopped listening to the naysayers around her. She decided she was going to do it differently. She did not want to be sixty-eight sitting in the same seat she was in now.

Without telling anyone, Janet applied to a local college. She did not want to tell anyone lest she not be accepted. But they accepted her. She began her studies. She was discouraged at first. She went to class with eighteen-year-olds who could have been her kids. She felt out of place and silly. She thought they were looking down on her.

Right before exams, the professor had the class split into study groups. It turned out everyone wanted to study with Janet. She had the stellar notes. She was the smart one. She knew best how to balance the challenges of college with the challenges of life. With each class, enrolling for the next became easier.

At work, Janet was quiet about her studies, but everyone started to notice changes in her. She had the look. She was happier. She was more confident. Her coworkers started to ask her questions, not only about work but about her. Had she met a man? Slowly she began to reveal her secret. Everyone was surprised. How did she find the time? How did she manage the kids? Was school difficult?

Until then, Janet had been exercising her spark. But when she started to share it with others, she began owning her divine plan. She began getting As. She began taking harder classes. She decided to get an MBA. She did not know where it would all lead, but she was no longer "just" a secretary.

The coeds, the coworkers, her family, even her boss,

were all inspired by Janet's commitment and devotion. It was not her intention to affect them, but she did just by following her divine path. The receptionist began the process of leaving an abusive marriage. One of Janet's study partners decided to move out of his parents' house. Even her best friend decided to go back to school. Janet became a catalyst without ever saying a word. Her divine spark was lighting the path for others.

Today, Janet is finishing her MBA. She is unsure where it will lead, but she can already see the profound changes within her and around her. Her children have become passionate about their studies. When Janet embraced her divine path, she became a better Janet, a better mother, a better daughter, a better friend. She realized this is what God dreamed for her.

What she did not know at the time was that I reviewed her best friend's college essay. It asked the applicant to discuss her inspiration. Janet was hers. Janet had no concept of the effects that her actions would have on others. At age thirty-eight, she was not trying to change the world, she was just trying to change herself.

In Judaism, we are commanded to tikkun olam, repair the world. It seems like an impossible task. Who am I to change the entire world? Who am I to fix the problems that exist?

You are God's agent. The first step in tikkun olam is tikkun bayit. Literally, repairing your house. When you heal your home, yourself, you are beginning to change the whole world.

The Talmud teaches that if you save a life, you save the world. The Talmud is not only referring to the person who dives under the train. The Talmud is referring to Janet. A person who saves herself.

The Talmud is referring to you. When you find your spark, partner with God, and bring it to the world, you change yourself and everything and everyone around you. You make the world better. You better all of God's creations.

> *Whose divine light inspires yours?*
> *Whose sparks are you making brighter?*

I Will Be What I Will Be

One of my favorite verses in the entire Torah is when Moses asked God, "What is your Name?"

Of course Moses did not expect the answer to be "George," but when God responded, "Ehyeh-Asher-Ehyeh, I will be what I will be," Moses knew that God was not content to stay put. God was not finished. God saw himself as a work in progress.

We must see ourselves as works in progress too. The Talmud teaches us, "For a person to be like God, he must be a partner in the act of creation." Each day you bring your light to the world, partner with God, and further creation, your position shifts.

You are acting instead of reacting. You are leading instead of following. You are asserting, not submitting. You are active, not passive. You are no longer just a mom. You are a creation of God, and you, just like God, may have seventy names. Mother, artist, teacher, creator, lover, friend, runner, wife, giver, the list goes on and on.

You no longer can be inert, because you are divine

and the world needs you to bring your divinity to it. The Kabbalists believe that we become truly connected to God when we unite our sparks with the sparks of other human beings. So too when you light your soul and enable others to do the same, you may find yourself, your partner, and true synergy with God.

Samantha had a list of all the things that she wanted in a man. Someone who cooks, travels, loves dogs, and does not mind entertaining. She always talked about starting her own bed-and-breakfast once she met the man. But she had not met him. So finally she decided, enough waiting for Prince Charming, she was going to start her own B & B. Within six months, an adorable man booked a stay for one night. Sparks flew, and he never left. Today they run the B & B together, pursuing their passion, living their dreams, and finding true love. When sparks fly, you never know what or whom they will touch.

You will be what you will be.

We Plan, God Laughs

LAUGHING WITH GOD

I am not sure how it all ends for me, for my mother, for you. God does not know either.

I will be what I will be.

People always ask me, "What happens when I die?" I wish I had an answer. As a rabbi, I have been with many people right before they died, holding their hands as they took their last breaths. I wish I could have comforted them with what lies ahead. It would have comforted me as well. I don't know.

But there is a mashal, a little story, that sheds light on the path.

When I die, I will meet God at the pearly gates. There God will ask me, "Were you the best Sherre Hirsch you could be?" God will not ask me, "Did all your dreams come true? Did you make a lot of money? Did you become famous?" God will not ask me why I was not Moses, Mother Teresa, or my mom. God will want to know if I was *me*—divine, authentic, extraordinary, regular me.

I hope I will be able to say yes. Then God and I will laugh together.

EPILOGUE

Today is not turning out like I imagined when I wrote the first line of this book. Even though I knew that things don't go as planned when I first said it, it still continues to surprise me. But "we plan, God laughs" moments never end.

My son did not get into the only kindergarten we applied to.

My youngest child did not walk until twenty-three months.

My mother was diagnosed with brain cancer.

Maybe part of me hoped that having had my share of family challenges that I had reached my quota. I would have other challenges, but not family ones. I planned, against my best advice, certain generalities.

Epilogue

My maternal grandmother died at ninety-seven. I planned that my mother would live as long and that she would get to see her grandchildren grow up. She would be at bar mitzvahs, weddings, even witness the birth of her great-grandchildren just as my grandmother did.

My mother planned in the same way. She planned to travel with her husband to Europe. She planned to spend time with her friends and family. She did not plan on brain surgery, chemotherapy, and radiation. She did not plan on having to be so courageous again. Hadn't she me her quota?

We plan, God laughs. Once again, I find myself struggling with God. I am sad, angry, and fearful. I am trying to find a way to take my own advice. I am trying to be on the same team with God once again. And the truth is that I need too. The last time I bore witness to my mother's courage, I was young. Now I am the married mother of three. I have changed careers, changed houses and my hair color. I am not the same person that I was when I was young or that I was the day before she was diagnosed.

A friend suggested that I re-read my book. "What happened?" is exactly what I was asking myself. What happened to the life I envisioned now that I have written the book? It is being replaced by doctor's appointments and ER visits. This is not the life I planned.

I find myself looking at my watch more frequently. I want to remind myself to be present. The present is scary, but the future is unknown and terrifying. When I wrote the book, I had forgotten that being in the present can be as painful as staying in the past. Sometimes the present is not where you want to be. But in those moments I remind myself, it is the only place that God and I can work together.

I need God to be my partner more than ever. I feel alone. Even while I am surrounded by people who love me and whom I love, I still feel alone. My mother and I have switched roles and I don't feel like I'm ready. She cared for me, now I care for her. Who will be my mom now? Part of me feels so young and part of me feels so old. It is a place I've never been and I do not like it. So I have been pulling away from God. If I'd had the choice, I would have cancelled the High Holidays altogether. Rather than spending the first day of Rosh Hashanah in synagogue, I spent it at the hospital.

I expected that as I pulled away God would be on the other side of the rope, trying to pull me back. A cosmic tug-of-war. But that's not what happened—

instead it feels like the harder I pull away from God, the faster I fall into God's lap from exhaustion. So what am I pulling? What is on the other end?

In this place of powerlessness, fear and sadness, I feel like I've got to pull. Pulling makes me feel like I'm doing something to hold onto a semblance of control when I have none. I am fooling myself. When I pull away from God, I get lucky—I fall right into God's lap. As I pull away from my husband, my children, my mother, I am lucky that they understand—for now.

But I have to move forward. I have to trust the partnerships, all of them. I have to trust that while there may not be a "happy ending" that with God I will laugh again.